Sign Here

The enterprise guide to closing contracts quickly

Second Edition

Alex Hamilton

Praise for *Sign Here*

Even high-end law firms don't have much advice they can offer a competent inhouse lawyer or GC on how to run their contract processes. But Radiant Law is much more than a law firm and Alex is much more than a lawyer. Read this book for insightful, well grounded, incremental, and practical advice on how to solve the Contracting Problem.

– Martin Clausen, former General Counsel of Maersk Line and Managing Director of Syngrato

Alex Hamilton is a compelling voice in contracts. He recognizes that fixing the systemic dysfunction requires establishing new incentives and overhauling the different components of the process. With Sign Here, he guides you through what's required in an insightful and accessible way. It's a unique resource.

– Ken Adams, Author of A Manual of Style For Contract Drafting

Excellent. well written, interesting conceptually and practically. A reminder that for all the lawtech hype we need to understand and engineer the service before we harp on about magic bullets.

– Professor Richard Moorhead

Essential reading for anyone involved in the contracting process - Alex is one of a few genuinely disruptive thinkers in the legal industry.

– Paul Boyle, Group Deputy General Counsel, Serco Plc

Alex shares his experience as a successful transactional lawyer and a master of the contracting process in the best possible way—by breaking down first principles and offering pragmatic, battle-tested solutions.

– Sol Irvine, former General Counsel at Concertiv and Partner, Yuson & Irvine

In my work with general counsel globally, they fall into two categories when thinking about contracts and contract management – where do I begin? or jumping too quickly to fix a small part of the problem. ***Sign Here*** provides a comprehensive and holistic view of how to assess needs and success in managing and closing contracts, faster. It provides much discipline and practical insight in a field that is crowded with failed attempts.

– Duc V. Trang, Head - Talent & Workforce Management at BriefBox, formerly Managing Director at Major, Lindsey & Africa and General Counsel and author of Architecture of Deals: Strategies for Transactional Lawyering

In my experience, most attorneys believe that contracting is broken. Unfortunately, they also believe that there is no way to fix it (a comfortable though not helpful posture). Alex's new book colorfully validates the first belief and systematically dismantles the second. This is a must read for anyone who is serious about contracting.

– Michael Naughton, Vice President xMentium, previously Director of Legal Service Innovation at Cisco

So much of the effort to fix broken contracting, adds complexity and cost without addressing the real fundamental issues. Alex Hamilton does it differently, going to the core of the problem and offering real-life solutions that are proven to work. Sign Here is a no-nonsense, hype-free, practical, relationships-first and thankfully brief guide on how to do it all - templates, process, negotiations, tech, data - better.

– Denis Potemkin, Head of Innovation at LexSolutions and founder of Majoto

I said it of the first edition and I will say it again. Don't come complaining to me about contracting before you read this. Life gets easier once you just listen to Alex.

– Elizabeth de Sadler, Director of Rehabilitated Lawyer, Novcon, and Hey Plain Jane

First published in Great Britain in 2021. Second edition published in Great Britain in 2024.

Alas, reading this book does not make Alex your lawyer.

v 2.0.1

ISBN 978-1-9196416-4-5

To Vita and Ada

Contents

Introduction to the second edition

Let's be honest with each other. I wrote this book because I want you to buy services from Radiant Law. You are probably reading this book because you want the solution on a plate, and you don't really want to buy anything from anyone.

That's OK.

When I wrote the first edition, I broke a simple rule: don't give the answer. Books written by businesses are meant to show you your problem and then only dangle the hint of a solution. That didn't feel right—not very "Radiant"—so I tried to make the book as practicable as possible.

However, my father, after reading the book, called me out on what I was really doing. I was setting out the problem, giving the solution, and relying on you to decide that there was too much involved to do it all yourself, so you would use Radiant Law anyway. Busted... yet the steps I set out are still needed if you want your contracting to fly.

Some readers hired us (we've doubled in size and opened in Trinidad and Malaysia to provide a global contracting service), some did it themselves, and some probably just continued the way they always have. I did receive some very kind feedback—thank you.

So why write a new version?

Contract Lifecycle Management systems became all the rage, and this bothered me for reasons I will explain. Then generative AI arrived, and some are declaring a new era. Is a book pre-dating GPT-4 old hat? We shall see.

Sign Here

There is much noise in the market about shiny things, but still too little discussion about what really matters. This feels like the time to double down on purpose and behaviour. I'm happy to die on the hill of the importance of relationships and I want to strengthen the message of the book.

Amongst the noise, the Radiant Law team has been figuring out new ways to improve contracting. Writing is how I clarify my thinking, and updating this book is my way of making sense of what we have been working on over the past three years. You should know them if you are doing it yourself.

A few things are different this time. This edition continues to be available on Amazon, but there is also a free PDF version on our website. You will also find the main changes in the second edition, to save you from having to read the whole book if you read the first edition.

There may need to be another edition in a few more years. GPT-8 might just be the knockout blow. But I suspect I will still be rooting for creating wonderful commercial relationships between humans.

In the meantime, if you do need help with your high-volume contracts, then please get in touch. Or just ask me a question—I want contracting to improve for everyone, including those doing it themselves.

21 May 2024

Introduction

Ten years ago, I did something foolish.

Up to then, I'd had a perfectly normal—bordering on successful—career in law. I'd made partner at a large American firm, was qualified in a couple of jurisdictions, and was known in my specialist area of outsourcing and technology deals… but I had an itch, and it was bothering me.

It seemed to me that there was something deeply wrong with how we were all approaching contracts. It had become a ritualised dance of predictable and often unreasonable positions taken by each side, heated arguments over irrelevant issues, with negotiations driven by "legal" points rather than substance. I was struck by how lawyers' incentives on these deals undermined the process—charging for time wasn't encouraging them to close deals quickly. Meanwhile, business leaders were looking on frustrated as contracts took far too long to complete, while the points they cared about most were being side-lined.

And so, in a moment of madness, I threw that stable career away and started Radiant Law, the first fixed-price law firm specialising in commercial contracts. We not only ditched the timesheet, but we also embraced technology and process improvements, using this as an opportunity to redesign how we delivered legal services.

Over the last ten years, the team at Radiant Law has done more than redesign legal services. With new incentives that encouraged us to get deals signed faster and the opportunity to support the day-to-day contracts of many of the largest companies in the world, we have been busy figuring out how to make contracting fly.

We knew from the beginning that we needed to look beyond the traditional world of contracting. We've worked with Lean[1], data analytics, and technology experts to create a new methodology for transforming contracting processes. The results we've achieved for our clients have been dramatic.

Ten years on, we're ready to share our methodology with you.

Who is this book for?

Every year, companies spend trillions of pounds buying goods and services from other companies. Underpinning every invoice for this spend is a contract. Commercial contracting[2] is a critical capability for every company.

Despite its importance, the typical contracting process tends to be document-centric, slow, and untouched by digitalisation. Companies are haemorrhaging value through mismanagement and racking up costs through unnecessary negotiations.

One of the challenges with contracting well is the number of departments involved and the lack of a clear owner. If ever there was an opportunity to create value at your company, fixing the end-to-end contracting process must be up there as a contender. Whether you're in legal, finance, sales, procurement, or the broader business, in many companies, there is an open goal for the person who steps up and seizes the opportunity to make contracting work better.

---

[1] Lean is the process improvement approach pioneered by Toyota. Originating in manufacturing, it has since been applied to services and is Radiant Law's core methodology for delivering continuous improvement, using the Shingo Model. As described by our advisor, Professor Norman Faull, "Lean is a system for creating thinking people."

[2] I refer to commercial contracts in this book, but the contents are just as applicable to finance, leasing, HR, and the many other contract types that your organisation will enter into each day.

This book is for that person. I'm going to show you where you need to start, what the building blocks are, how they fit together, how to apply automation, and how to introduce a continuous improvement process so your contracting keeps getting better.

Your company will be entering into many different types of contracts, from purchase orders to highly complex transactions. In this book, I will be focusing on the contracts that sit somewhere in the middle, the higher-volume negotiated agreements—your daily deals. Learnings will carry across to contracts at both extremes, but it's the middle that holds the most opportunities for standardisation and improvement.

What this book is not about is contracts themselves. I'm not going to cover how to draft, what should go into your agreement, nor how to negotiate. There won't be any law, and it won't matter where you are based. However, I have included a reading list at the end, which will point you to great resources on these topics.

Why do we have contracts?

Contracts don't look very attractive on your shelf, they don't taste nice, and they won't give you shelter—so what value do they add? The answer is that businesses need to work with others through commercial relationships. And the purpose of the contract is to help get those relationships going.

In other words, the objective of the contracting process is not to create contracts; it's to create and grow relationships. Contracts help us along the way by building confidence. They do this by giving the parties certainty about what the mutual promises are and that those promises will be kept (because there will, at least in theory, be some recourse if they aren't).

But if we're trying to create relationships, why are we so darn'd difficult with each other in negotiations? Why do we keep trying to start abusive relationships? And why are we so focused on what could go wrong rather than on how to make things go right?

How to fix contracting

We need to apply new thinking to fix contracting. We need to start relationships on the right foot. We need to treat contracting as a standardisable process and stop making it up as we go along. We need to recognise that there is no sweeping fix that will make everything alright and that instead, we will have to make lots of small changes to keep improving how we work. We need leaders who will make the process work across our organisations.

Building on these principles, we need to move to a better approach to contracting: RADICAL contracting:

Reasonable rather than maximal positions.

Automated rather than manual processes.

Data-driven rather than relying on folklore.

Incremental improvements rather than large-scale transformations.

Collaborative with the other side and across your organisation rather than adversarial and siloed.

Accelerated rather than ponderous.

Long-term relationships rather than short-term transactions.

I'm going to show you a structured approach to implementing RADICAL contracting using our 3Rs methodology so you can fix your contracting in three stages:

- **Repeatable**: Standardising your contracting process, including putting the core templates and tools in place, ready to be improved.

- **Robots**: Applying cost-effective and straightforward technology that works.

- **Refinement**: Implementing a continuous improvement process that keeps enhancing your contract terms and contracting process to focus on your stakeholders' needs.

There will be lots of different pieces to the puzzle that you will be putting in place at each stage of the 3Rs methodology, and I'm going to walk you through each of these stages step by step:

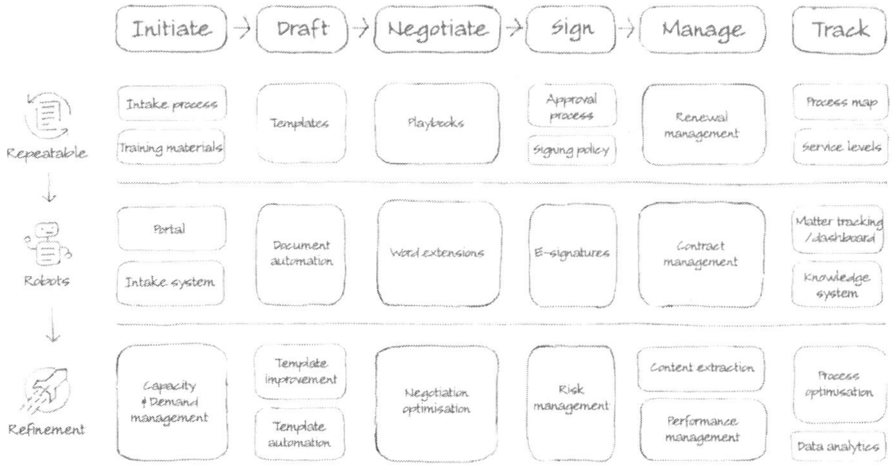

Figure 1 - 3Rs: the full map

The 3Rs methodology will transform your contracting by:

- speeding up your time to close contracts,

- ensuring that you are using the right people to support your contracting,

- reducing your cost-per-contract,
- improving the risk management of your contracting portfolio, and
- delivering better business outcomes from your commercial relationships.

We're moving to an increasingly networked world, where no one company does everything itself for the end consumer. Building an ecosystem of companies around you to help create value will be a core business challenge of the 21st century, so contracting has never been more critical. Now is the time to establish a fantastic contracting process in your company that gives you the relationships and the competitive advantage you need to succeed.

Chapter 1 The Contracting Problem

As a contracting professional, it can be a salutary experience asking a typical business user what they think of the contracting process. From their perspective, contracting is often a hell hole of squabbling over minor points in unreadable documents that costs a fortune and takes forever. They know they need to get through it, but they hate the experience. I call this "the contracting problem".

In this chapter, I will explore the painful reality of contracting and some of its causes. We need to face this if we are going to do better.

Your contracts matter

Contracts matter. To understand why, just consider your company's profit and loss report. You can't send an invoice to a customer without a contract, so all revenue depends on contracts. You also can't get access to power, logistics, IT, or any of the other third-party services your company relies upon without a contract. Without contracts, you would have to build your own power station. Many, if not most, of the lines on your P&L relate to commercial agreements. Your company will inevitably also be partnering with others to achieve common goals.

Think about it from the perspective of your CEO. The typical CEO is probably prioritising: (1) growth, (2) leveraging technology and applying innovation, (3) making savings, (4) environmental, social, and governance issues, (5) dealing with regulatory change, and (6) people and culture. Commercial contracts relate to at least the first five of these six categories, and commercial relationships can often be intrinsic to success.

However, the world of commercial contracts is too often a mess. Why a mess? Let me give you some examples.

Problem 1: Contracts cost too much

World Commerce and Contracting (WorldCC) estimated in 2017[3] that the average company it surveyed was spending almost twice as much as a top-quartile company on getting its contracts in place. WorldCC found even a simple and low-risk contract cost, on average, an eye-watering £5,000 to complete for each party, which was almost 40% more expensive than six years earlier. 99% of organisations[4] understandably want to reduce their contracting costs, with a third aiming for cost savings of more than 30%.

This is despite legal work having migrated in-house, as law firms priced themselves out of the market. According to a Gartner benchmark in 2018[5], in-house teams review 75% of contracts. The benchmark goes on to offer a clue as to why it costs so much: only 3% of the surveyed legal departments had fully automated their commercial contracts process and 99% of organisations[6] were still saying in 2021 that they didn't have the data and technology they needed to improve their contracting processes.

Problem 2: Contracts take too long

We all know the experience of contract processes dragging on. Consider one figure from the Association of Corporate Counsel's

---

[3] Or $6,900, with complex contracts averaging at $50,000. A more recent study by WorldCC (Benchmark Report 2021) shows the typical range of costs are from 1.5% of the contract value for simple transactions, rising to 16% for complex transactions.

[4] 2021 EY Global Law Survey. This also included a forecast of a 25% increase in legal workloads while budgets shrink by 20%.

[5] Gartner's 2018 Legal Technology and Analytics Benchmarking Report.

[6] 2021 EY Global Law Survey.

2019 global legal department benchmarking report: the average time to review a contract is over 30 days[7].

The cost of these delays can go far beyond the cost of the contracting process itself. If a sales contract takes a long time to close, revenue is permanently lost, or at the least, cash arrives later. Similarly, if a procurement contract is delayed, the business value is postponed and may even evaporate. In one survey 94% of business development teams reported challenges with their contracting support, including slow turn-around times[8] and bureaucratic processes, with 57% saying it had resulted in delayed revenue recognition[9]. Speed is a necessity, not a luxury.

---

[7]ACC 2019 Benchmark Report.

[8] Turn-around times refers to how quickly a contract is drafted, or a red-line is responded to. Basically, how long is the contract sitting with the contract team before it can be sent back to the other side.

[9] 2021 EY Global Law Survey again. 50% of organisations in that survey also said that inefficiencies in the contracting processes had cost them business.

Case Study: The Split Test

In 2018, we helped four companies update their contracts to deal with new privacy legislation that was about to come into effect. We noticed that the four projects were taking wildly different times to complete—some were quick, while others dragged out:

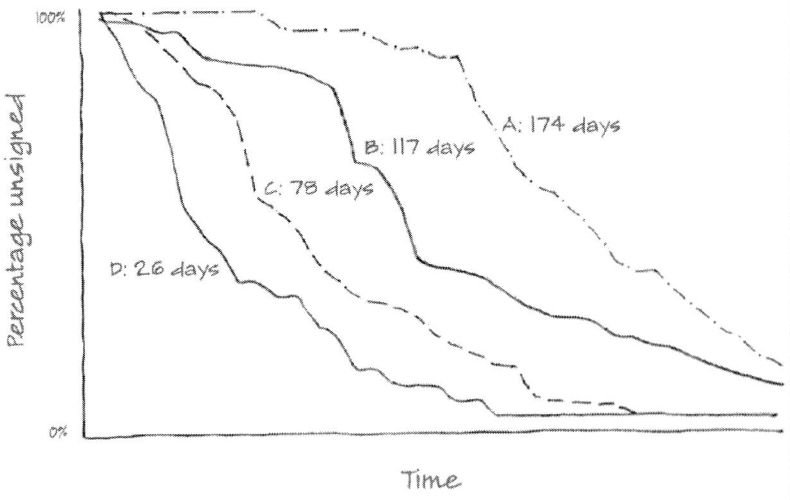

Figure 2 - Burn-down chart of projects

Project D was closing amendments almost seven times faster on average than Project A (26 days on average compared to 174 days).
The range was so surprising that we dug deeper. The team identified two differences between the projects: how good the clients were at getting approvals, signatures, etc. (unsurprisingly, large enterprises struggle) and how reasonable the first draft was (specified by the client). A statistical analysis suggested both factors were affecting the time to complete the projects.

The difference between Project B and Project D stood out. The only difference between the projects was one additional provision asked for by the Project B client to increase the other side's overall liability. That one provision (not required by the change in law) caused the average time to close an amendment to take over four times longer.

Case Study 1 – The Split Test [10]

Problem 3: Contracting hinders rather than helps relationships

Most of your day-to-day contracts will be relational rather than transactional[11]. There will be transactional contracts, too, ranging from simple spot sales to mergers and acquisitions, but the typical business contract covered by this book will start or grow a relationship. Relationships are indeed being created and grown, but successful relationships are often ***despite*** rather than ***because of*** the agreement.

Here are three ways this can play out in practice:

- **The contracting process undermines the relationship:** There are many ways to damage a relationship, but common examples include sending out unreasonable and trust-destroying first drafts; adversarial behaviours and use of leverage to maximise outcomes; positional rather than principle-led negotiations that don't maximise the opportunity; and using the contract after signing as a weapon rather than a baseline.

---

[10] A later analysis of fines by the data privacy regulator suggested that the liability change made by the Project B client was pointless. The types of data being processed were low risk and unlikely to be the subject of material fines, even if something went wrong.

[11] There are also "relational" contracts, where companies partner and the relationship is paramount. These contracts tend to fall at the most complex end of the spectrum and hence outside the main scope of this book. There is a resource on relational contracts in the reading list at the end. Hopefully, the developments in that field will be more widely applied across the contracting spectrum.

- **The negotiations focus on the wrong topics**: WorldCC carries out a regular survey of its global members, asking what gets negotiated and what goes wrong in practice[12]. For two decades, WorldCC has repeatedly found that negotiations focus on what happens when the contract goes completely awry (such as provisions covering liability limits, termination, and indemnities), while what goes wrong in practice is that the parties don't have a common understanding of scope and pricing. Too often, we set up our contracts to fail because we spend our time focusing on failure rather than the basics that would prevent the failure in the first place. It's a true self-fulfilling prophecy.

- **Relationship value leaks:** In another study[13], WorldCC found an average value erosion of 8.6% of contract value due to poor contracting practices. We are losing real money by not running our contracts well.

Problem 4: Contracting teams are overstretched

It's not just companies experiencing problems; the contracting teams[14] themselves are suffering.

---

[12] WorldCC Most Negotiated Terms 2022. Since the first edition, a new survey came out with little fundamental change: "Once more, the list of Most Negotiated Terms shows little change and remains dominated by time spent on risk allocation, rather than value creation. [...] When it comes to risk, many negotiators appear to have 'doubled down' in their wish to either impose or avoid the financial consequences of failure".

[13] WorldCC ROI of Contracting Excellence 2023. This is a (small) reduction from the 9.2% value erosion found in its initial study in 2014.

[14] I often refer to "contracting teams" in this book as they may be organisationally distinct to, or extend beyond, the legal team, but contracting teams usually at least include lawyers. Where I refer to the "business", I mean departments other

- Teams are struggling to deal with the day-to-day demand for contracts, let alone when volumes spike[15]. No wonder the average time to review an agreement is 30 days.

- Meanwhile, general counsels (GCs) are asked to do "more for less". Having delivered the initial saving of moving legal support in-house from expensive law firms, adding more heads is treated with hostility by CFOs[16].

- Contracting teams rarely find the time needed to improve[17], which is exacerbated by some thinking of change as needing to be transformational and ignoring opportunities for small, quick wins.

- This also means that contracting teams are spending too much time on tactical rather than strategic work, while struggling to demonstrate value to their organisation[18].

---

than the contracting team (but that doesn't mean the contracting team isn't part of the overall business).

[15] According to Radiant Law's Contracting Scorecard, 77% of in-house teams have moderate to material slowdowns when there are spikes in volumes.

[16] According to Gartner's 2021 Legal Planning & Budgeting report, only 6% of in-house teams were expecting to increase headcount, while 20% were expecting to decrease headcount.

[17] The WorldCC Benchmark Survey 2023 found the highest barrier to progress was operational workload, followed by budget, and then "establishing data to demonstrate value and contribution". I wonder what would happen if teams reversed this list and started with a conversation about value.

[18] The EY Global Legal Survey 2021 found that high volumes of low complexity contracts were a challenge for 89% of respondents, with 54% saying they took away firm from more important tasks and 37% saying they lowered employee morale by making the team feel underutilised. The EY ACC Survey 2023 found

The missing pieces

This book contains many of the tools and actions needed to improve your contracting process (and why they matter). Most companies have taken only a few of these steps, which explains many of their problems. We know what happens in practice from collecting data for years through our scorecards. This is what the data tells us a typical company has done[19]:

- Although the company has a contracts-focused legal team, they can't do large, complex deals in-house[20].
- The company has templates for some but not all their common contracts, but they haven't automated them. The templates themselves are generally overly long, unreasonable and unclear[21].

---

that 70% of legal teams were spending more time on tactical rather than strategic work. 68% of respondents in the WorldCC Benchmark Report 2023 considered increasing strategic relevance and demonstrating value to be a high priority.

[19] The percentages in the notes for this section are based on the responses from 89 companies to Radiant Law's Contracting Scorecard, with the companies ranging from signing at least a hundred contracts a year to many thousands. It is hard to determine how good the sampling is: it might err towards companies with problems or companies showing off their improvements. I have supplemented the data with the WorldCC Benchmark Report 2023 and EY Global Law Survey 2021 where they cover the topic. These other surveys also suggest that many companies have much room for improvement. There are undoubtedly companies with great contracting processes, but we are seeing only a small proportion in the data who have put most of the steps in place and whose processes are flying.

[20] Although 91% have a contracts legal team, only 31% can handle most strategic deals in-house.

[21] We found that only 12% have templates for all the contracts that the business could create. 51% have some standard templates for the legal team, but only 11%

- They've started making materials and training available to the business, but it's haphazard[22].

- The business tends to ask their favourite lawyer for help rather than using a centralised intake process. In any case, there are probably no service levels in place for how fast the contracting team will respond to requests for help (and even if service levels do exist, they are unlikely to be measured). Nor are there rules of engagement for requests, with the business often appearing with urgent requests then disappearing for months[23].

- If there is a playbook for negotiation positions, it only covers a few issues and hasn't been updated recently (or goes on for a hundred pages and is unusable)[24].

---

have unified templates with consistent terms and only 13% have a style guide. These numbers have improved with the WorldCC report finding 92% of organisations now have at least some contract templates, although only 50% have begun to simplify their templates. The EY survey found that 69% didn't require their team to only use preapproved templates. We found that 26% have started to automate their templates, but only 4% have automated all their templates. WorldCC found 27% have put template-based document automation in place (and 21% clause-based document automation, but these systems can overlap), but didn't report on how much actual automation had occurred. The EY survey found 36% were using document automation.

[22] 79% have run occasional training sessions for the business, but only 11% run a training programme.

[23] We found 56% have not put in place a central place to send requests. 32% have service levels for responding but only 11% track whether they are meeting the service level. WorldCC found only 32% had put in place online intake forms.

[24] We found 51% have playbooks, but only 11% consider theirs to be comprehensive and regularly updated. The EY survey found that only 31% of organisations were using playbooks.

- Electronic signatures are the one technology that has been introduced somewhere in the organisation[25].

- The company either stores its contracts in an online folder or in a contract management system with haphazard data. It will often not be able to lay its hands on a signed version or know whether it has been amended[26].

- The contracting process will be being tracked manually, if at all, with little data and no analysis. The contracting team often can't tell you how many contracts they are supporting each year[27].

- The contracting team will also be overstretched, only able to get to improvements haphazardly[28].

In short, the typical company is still light on tools, technology, data, and process.

---

[25] This improved significantly in the pandemic. The EY survey found that 84% are using electronic signatures.

[26] We found 47% use a contract management system, but only 19% systematically track metadata and 20% proactively manage contract performance. WorldCC found that 62% had a contract repository but the EY survey had 90% of respondents saying they faced challenges trying to locate contracts and 49% not having a defined process for storing contracts after execution.

[27] We found only 25% consistently track progress of matters, 16% use a tracking system (as opposed to a shared document). The EY survey found 28% using workflow tools, WorldCC found 18%.

[28] Only 13% are running an ongoing improvement programme (as opposed to ad hoc efforts), and only 4% are using data to inform that programme.

When we talk to teams about their progress, they regularly tell us they fear they're behind their peers at other companies. The good news is that they are often not behind; the bad news is it's because so many of their peers are doing poorly.

Three perverse incentives

"***Never, ever think about anything else when you should be thinking about the power of incentives.***" – Charlie Munger

Some particularly perverse incentives are worth bearing in mind as you try to fix your contracting processes:

Protecting relevance

You may have noticed that some participants seem to make things more complicated than they should be. They may also appear to squirrel away knowledge. This behaviour often stems from a fear that their job will be at risk if everyone finds out that their part in the process isn't exactly rocket science.

Interestingly, participants are often quick to point out that the role of the person down the corridor is blindingly simple, whereas theirs is particularly hard. Funnily enough, if you ask the other person, they might have a similar perspective, except that it's their role that's particularly hard.

Let's be honest: except for a few tricky types of deals, there's nothing associated with the contracting process that's that complicated. The law isn't so hard; any of the points that come up are perfectly understandable by a moderately bright participant. Even the technology involved is rather banal (as we'll see later, despite all the talk of AI, it's mainly just databases, workflow, and document transformations).

What's hard is cutting through all the noise to make things simple. If you see someone creating a ton of complexity, they're not doing a great job. You may need to reassure them that they will still have a job if they help make the process go faster, not slower.

The good news is that anyone adept at simplifying things will be precious to their employer. The even better news for experienced team members is that if they can make the work more straightforward, it can be supported by more junior team members or suppliers, freeing them up to work on the more strategic and exciting deals.

Playing safe

Your average CEO doesn't wake up every morning wondering how to crush all risk out of existence. They're often looking for chances to take on more risk in a clever way as they try to grow the company and take advantage of opportunities.

But by the time you get down to the line workers, the overriding concern is often to avoid being accused later of missing something or doing something wrong. This tendency shows itself in the unreasonable standard templates that companies too often use and how they behave in negotiations.

Some business cultures have finger-pointing far too embedded to expect participants to act in any other way. In others, though, it's a question of whether leaders will provide support.

Clocking up hours

Not entirely unconnected to the above is the billable hour's impact, which is one of the most effective ways to get intelligent people to play dumb. Unfortunately, this system is deeply entrenched in most law firms.

The billable hour drives up complexity and slows down transactions. Why send a reasonable draft when you can send something one-sided that will inspire an unreasonable response and hence increase the time spent battling back to some middle ground? Why simplify processes if you can't charge as much? And why use automation that gets rid of billable hours?

At Radiant Law, we know that if a law firm is involved on the other side of a negotiation, it will take three to five times longer to close a contract than when it's an in-house team (who aren't incentivised to drag the matter out). We avoided timesheets from day one because we knew they would incentivise team members to make things more complicated. By only charging on a fixed-price basis, we were instead incentivised to speed up our clients' contracts.

The easy solution to this problem is to stop buying time from your law firm and ensure that they aren't incentivising the people working on your deals to make them overly complex. It's incredible how behaviours will change when you fix this[29].

Summary

Contracting excellence is becoming increasingly critical to business success, but generally, we aren't doing it well. Contracts typically take too long and cost too much to put in place, and the contracting process and contracts themselves are too often not setting organisations up for relationship success. The teams responsible for the contracting process tend to be overstretched and struggling to implement change while facing ongoing budgetary pressures.

---

[29] Unfortunately, even when billable hour incentives aren't in play, lawyers (whether external or internal) do tend to make things more complex than necessary. Getting rid of the billable hour helps but doesn't solve everything.

In practice, though, most teams haven't put in place many of the basics that can help solve these issues. Meanwhile, perverse incentives, such as fears of redundancy and finger-pointing, and the billable hour are hindering progress.

The good news is that all of this is fixable and there is a better way. Some ground-breaking companies have figured out how to increase productivity, reduce costs, speed up the contracting process, and create happy customers and suppliers, as well as a happy contracting team. Time to find out how they do that.

Chapter 2 Rethinking Contracting

The problems in the contracting process can feel so embedded that change seems impossible. Change is possible, but you need to apply new thinking to the issues.

In this chapter, I'm going to explore four principles that are crucial to delivering a better contracting process:

- contracting should foster great relationships,
- contracting is a standardisable process,
- there is no silver bullet, and
- fixing contracting requires leadership.

Building on these fundamental principles, I will then introduce the RADICAL approach to contracting and the 3Rs improvement methodology.

Principle 1: Contracting should foster great relationships

"Contract law is essentially a defensive scorched-earth battleground where the constant question is, 'if my business partner was possessed by a brain-eating monster from beyond spacetime tomorrow, what is the worst thing they could do to me?'" - Charles Stross

The purpose of contracting is to create commercial relationships. It's the relationship that creates the value, not the contract, because it's the relationship that delivers what each party needs.

We may talk in terms of companies contracting with each other, but companies are a legal fiction. Commercial relationships are built on relationships between people. It's the people on each side who trust or don't trust the other side, make the decisions that determine whether the relationship grows or founders, and do the work that creates the value for each party. It is ultimately also people who profit from the value created by the relationship. You can't treat the commercial relationship of two organisations as distinct from the relationships between the people on each side, and the success of the commercial relationship will depend on the behaviour of people.

There is another dimension to personal relationships and RADICAL contracting: Contracting is cross-departmental, and decisions can't just be handed down to all the participants, so you will need to influence others and that too requires building relationships. Change requires collaboration, and collaboration is built on personal relationships.

It is no coincidence that Radiant Law's purpose is to "create great relationships". It is the heart of not only what we are trying to achieve for our clients but how we need to work with our clients and between our team members, to get things done.

If relationships are core both to what we are trying to achieve with contracting, and how we improve contracting, then we need to talk about trust, because trust is foundational to relationships. Contracting is an exercise in trust building with the other party. Influencing your peers in your organisation to make the changes described in this book also requires building trust.

Unfortunately, we can't magic up trust by asking others to "trust us" —that is instead an excellent way to destroy trust. Creating trust requires us to act trustworthily, in other words it is about how we behave.

What does trustworthy mean? David Maister et al[30] gave a helpful formula for trust in personal business interactions:

$$\textbf{Trustworthiness} = \frac{\textbf{Credibility + Reliability + Intimacy}}{\textbf{Self-orientation}}$$

Where **credibility** means you being perceived as knowing a topic or being able to do something; **reliability** means you have a track record of delivering what you said you would do; **intimacy** means creating a sense of safety and security in the other person; and **self-orientation** means the extent to which you put your interests first. The more you focus on your own interests rather than the other person's, the less you will be trusted.

Intimacy, a word that makes many lawyers uncomfortable, is particularly important. To create value for someone else requires that you understand what they need and are willing to help them achieve it. This requires two additional points that Edgar Schein highlighted[31]. The first is curiosity: being genuinely interested in the other person, their situation and motivations, and what they need. The other is being willing to share appropriate information about oneself, to open up and trust the other person, and in turn encourage them to share. The act of trusting can itself help create trust.

---

[30] From the book The Trusted Advisor by David H. Maister, Robert Galford, and Charles Green.

[31] From his book on coaching, Humble Inquiry.

We have the elements coming together for both relationships between organisations as well as between people at your organisation: openness, curiosity, a focus on the other person, doing what you say, being able to do what you say, and being willing to prioritise the others interests. This is not easy, but without trust we cannot build great relationships, and relationships are how we can get things done.

Let's bring this back to contracting and the behaviour we show during the contracting process. Successful negotiations that build trust and create value for both parties require that we focus on not just our own objectives, but also the other party's. What does that look like?

Initiation

- Working with your business team to understand what they are trying to achieve early in the deal and helping them think through how it might best work.

- Sending short, clear, reasonable, and relevant first drafts, which reflect the likely (or if known, actual) objectives of the other party as well as your organisation's.

Negotiations

- Helping focus the contract discussions on what is essential to successful delivery and long-term sustainability, instead of concentrating on liability if it goes wrong.

- Adopting a principle-led negotiation style[32], trying to grow the value of the future relationship for both parties by

---

[32] As argued for in Fisher, Ury, and Patton's brilliant book Getting to Yes.

exploring in negotiations the other party's objectives and how they might be achieved, while also sharing your own objectives.

- Using negotiations as an opportunity to create personal relationships both with the wider team at your organisation and with the team at the other party.

- Being open about where there are challenges and risks, and working with the other party and your team to find solutions that minimise their impact; not just sticking the risk on the other side if they do not have control.

- Being aware of cultural differences, especially during international negotiations, and being sensitive to other approaches and adapting your personal style.

- Not acting like a bully, even when you have a much stronger negotiating position, and instead working to ensure that both parties consider the outcome a success.

- Ensuring that team members are consulted with and informed of progress, and that stakeholder needs are being met and not lost sight of.

- Ensuring that you only agree in the negotiation to do things that your organisation is confident that it can deliver.

Relationship Management

- Ensuring that the people at your organisation who will need to deliver the deal, know what has been agreed to (and can understand the contract!).

- Actively managing the relationship, using the contract as a baseline but recognising that the deal may need to evolve as circumstances change.

- Looking for opportunities to grow the relationship and create more value for both parties, erring on the side of long-term sustainability rather than short-term wins.

- Sharing concerns, giving early warnings of issues, and showing flexibility and acting collaboratively in addressing challenges.

Finally, trust can be lost quickly. Any moment of putting your interests first or being oblivious to others' needs will undermine trust. So consistency throughout the negotiation process and beyond is essential. It is not enough to try to fix things when negotiations are struggling. We need to start, from the very first interaction, to try to help both parties achieve their objectives.

Principle 2: Contracting is a standardisable process

"***If you can't describe what you are doing as a process, you don't know what you're doing.***" - W. Edwards Deming

Every deal is different, but the question to ask is how different? Traditionally, contracting has been handled in a somewhat haphazard manner, emphasising bespoke agreements and a process that is more art than science. But if you take a step back and look at the bigger picture, there is a natural sequence to what needs to be done, which people generally follow. Do it long enough, and you'll know what issues are likely to come up. Yes, there will always be outlier deals where everything breaks down, and the other side manages to turn what should take a few days or weeks into many months of hell, but these are the exception, not the rule[33].

If we focus on standardising the "happy path", as programmers call it, and treat the "deals gone bad" as the exception and not the norm[34], then we have a chance to make progress.

Many advantages come from standardisation of the process:

- it's easier to teach the process to more junior members of your team and develop their skills if you have a clear and well-documented approach,
- you'll reduce variability, helping make the process cheaper and faster while increasing quality and predictability[35],
- your team will have to spend less time on the mechanical parts (and the mechanical parts will be more readily automated), making the work more engaging and your team more productive, and
- only once things are standardised can you start systematically improving them.

---

[33] In our experience, these account for less than 10% of small to medium-sized deals if you start with short, clear, reasonable, and relevant terms.

[34] Deals gone bad are, however, an excellent source of learning for how to improve the process and minimise their occurrence in the future.

[35] Reducing variability is a core concept in applying Lean to improve outcomes. For more on standardising work (and the connected need to level work), see the books in the reading list on Lean.

This last point is crucial. You need a single, documented way of working to collect data and tell whether a future change is an improvement or a step backwards.

Another aspect of standardisation is recognising that contracting is a well-understood discipline. Although many companies haven't finished putting the basics in place, the things you need to do and what works are predictable, and I spell them out in this book. You also don't need to reinvent the wheel. You will need to make standard solutions work for your circumstances, but generally, your approach will have strong similarities with other high-performing companies. "Happy families are all alike," as Tolstoy observed.

Principle 3: There is no silver bullet

"Of all the monsters who fill the nightmares of our folklore, none terrify more than werewolves because they transform unexpectedly from the familiar into horrors. For those, we seek bullets of silver that can magically lay them to rest." – Frederick P. Brooks Jr.[36]

Contrary to the enthusiastic presentations from legal tech providers that you have no doubt seen, there is, alas, no single system or improvement that will solve all your contracting issues. Why is this?

- We are dealing with messy humans and all their emotions and needs. However neatly we want them to fit into a perfectly automated system, it's never that simple.

[36] From Frederick P. Brooks Jr's brilliant essay No Silver Bullet – Essence and Accident in Software Engineering where he argued in 1987 that there was no single development in either technology or management technique that could transform productivity, reliability, or simplicity in software development within a decade.

- We are also dealing with the vast complexity of the real world, where commercial contracts bite. As much as we want to describe the world with taxonomies and pre-set options, exceptions always appear in practice.

- As I describe in this book, there are many aspects to improving contracting. Trying to solve them all in one swoop would mean taking on a complex, risky and expensive transformation, even with the improbable assumption of having sufficient information about what will work in advance.

So, while it is very human and understandable to wish it weren't so, there is no silver bullet that will solve everything. This is true of contract lifecycle management software, which was the rebranding that marketing departments at software companies came up with when adding features to cover each contracting process stage. This is true of artificial intelligence, even generative AI. This is true of blockchain, which has little to add to contracts that a database couldn't better handle. This is true of robotic process automation (RPA), a way of gluing together antiquated systems. And it's true of anything labelled "next generation"[37].

Instead of a silver bullet, think in terms of a silver shotgun cartridge (or shell)—make lots of small changes rather than one big change. Try something, see if it works, embrace it if it does, and repeat.

You might find it depressing to discover that there is no single solution and that what you suspected to be snake oil is snake oil, but there is good news here, too: because many changes can be

[37] The closest thing we have to a silver bullet is a short, clear, reasonable, and relevant contract template. This has a disproportionate impact on time to close, and the best bang for your bucks in improving your contracting.

made as relatively small tweaks, they can also be cheap, fast, and low risk.

Principle 4: Fixing contracting requires leadership and a team

"Leadership is not a position or a title, it is action and example." – Donald McGannon.

Contracting is a highly cross-functional activity (or at least it should be). Just within one party, and even for a more straightforward contract, you could have sales or procurement, operations, finance, regulatory, and possibly other specialist departments involved[38]. This raises a couple of challenges:

- First, contracting is inherently more complicated to fix than a process contained within one department. Often, hand-offs are messy, responsibilities are not clearly defined, and the list of stakeholders is vague.

- Second, you probably won't find a chief contracts officer in the C-suite, so who is the contracting process leader in your organisation[39]?

It is common, especially in larger companies, for participants to stick to their part of the contract, with no one leading the improvement of the overall process. But this is a missed

[38] WorldCC Benchmark Report 2023 reported that 29% of the average organisation's workforce were involved in some way in the contracting process.

[39] Curiously, the EY Global Law Survey 2021 found that 59% of legal teams, 56% of contracting teams, and 39% of business development teams all thought they were leading contracting. Despite these departmental claims, we continue to see a dearth of leadership.

opportunity. For the bold, there is a real chance to add demonstrable business value by stepping up.

Leadership is required to create a functioning and coherent end-to-end process. It would be best, though, to err on the side of collaboration and coordination rather than command and control, and anyone proposing to do this would do well to get their own house in order first.

Leadership is also nothing without a team. You will not only need to bring others with you, but you will also need access to a wide range of skills. No one person in your organisation is likely to have all the skills necessary to truly fix contracting, especially given all the disciplines that turn out to be so relevant, such as legal, design, project management, data analytics, process improvement, and so on.

There are, however, many ways to get access to these skills, including in the legal operations corners of larger legal teams and from third-party suppliers (especially the less traditional ones) and other departments within your organisation.

I also believe that participants in the process, including the lawyers, could learn new skills if they were, heaven forbid, to read broadly. This view, sometimes espoused as the "T-shaped"[40] professional, suggests that although you need to bring a core expertise to sit at the table (the vertical stroke of the T), you add more value through a broader but shallower understanding of many other topics (the horizontal stroke). If a little knowledge is a dangerous thing, then

[40] There are other variations of this idea, including O-shaped and Delta-shaped lawyers. We've seen a strong update of the O-shaped model in legal departments at least in the UK, which is encouraging. See https://www.oshaped.com/ and https://www.lawdeltamodel.com/

just read more! It's probably easier for someone with a deep understanding of the contracting process to learn other skills than for an expert in another discipline to absorb the nuances of contracting.

Introducing RADICAL contracting

Building on these principles (focusing on creating great relationships, standardising the process, accepting there are no silver bullets, and recognising the need for leadership and a team) brings us to Radiant Law's approach: RADICAL contracting. At its heart, RADICAL contracting focuses on creating quick, simple processes that prioritise what matters, relies on empiricism rather than opinion for improvements, and seeks to achieve good enough results with the other side to allow the relationship to get going.

Here is a summary of how RADICAL contracting compares to the traditional approach to contracting:

Traditional approach	RADICAL approach
Maximal positions	Reasonable positions
Manual	Automated
Folklore	Data-driven
Big bang or stasis	Improving iteratively
Adversarial	Collaborative
Ponderous	Accelerated
Transactional relationships	Long-term relationships

Reasonable positions

Companies often adopt a maximalist approach in their contracts, trying to win as much as possible on every point rather than being reasonable and heading straight to the middle ground. This might be appropriate for the most critical points in the deal (anchoring can work[41]), but I consider this a fundamental mistake when applied generally across the contract:

- **Speed to close**: Unreasonable terms create negotiations that slow down signing the agreement, reducing its value.

- **Losing deals**: Unreasonable terms can even kill deals. The other side may engage to see if you are serious, but if you continue to insist on your positions, they might walk away[42].

- **Winning the wrong points**: Unreasonable positions on topics that are not central to the contract yield little value.

- **Long-term deals need to be reasonable**: For a long-term relationship to work, both sides need to feel good about the negotiation outcome long after it has been signed.

- **Inviting retaliation**: Even if you are the overwhelmingly dominant partner, you still need the other side to cooperate over the long term, as there will often be opportunities for retaliation.

---

[41] Anchoring is when you make the first offer in a negotiation, which has been shown by psychologists Daniel Kahneman and Amos Tversky to tend to change the behaviour of the other side and pull them towards the initial offer. See these Harvard articles for more on the topic:
https://www.pon.harvard.edu/tag/anchoring-in-negotiation/

[42] Case in point: when writing this book, I planned to use a publishing house that claimed publicly to have highly reasonable terms. When they sent the actual contract, this turned out not to be the case, and when asked to change the most egregious points, they refused. I turned to Kindle Direct Publishing (Amazon has been busy disrupting the publishing industry) and a brilliant team of helpers found through Upwork. Unreasonable contracts can have real-world effects.

Unreasonable starting positions beget unreasonable responses. In contrast, the response to reasonable terms is typically just to accept them or raise minor points (although that's especially the case if you have an in-house lawyer on the other side[43]). In any event, you can always say no to unreasonable responses and hold your ground, so even if you get an unusually unreasonable reaction, it doesn't mean that you must go backwards.

The model we espouse is sending out terms that you would be OK signing as-is if you were on the other side. Reasonable positions represent the likely outcome if two well-advised parties hammered out a compromise that they could both live with. This is far from "giving the farm away", and the positions should reflect your needs as well as those of the other side.

I acknowledge this approach is controversial because it requires giving up potential gains that would come if the other side capitulated. My argument is that these potential gains are generally not that valuable in practice. The value of closing contracts quicker and getting going earlier more often outweighs possible gains from protracted negotiations[44]. I have also frequently seen what happens

---

[43] As mentioned in Chapter 1, our experience is that deals involving an external law firm will, on average, take three to five times longer to close. The delay is particularly exacerbated when the external lawyer doesn't regularly negotiate the relevant type of contract. The counterexample is that a highly experienced external lawyer is more likely to focus on what matters and cut to the chase—you just don't see them often in day-to-day deals.

[44] Try to identify how many times your company has had material disputes about its contracts in the past ten years and, of those disputes, how many turned on the nuance of a particular clause. We ask this regularly of clients, and they have consistently had so few examples (most often none) that it has been impossible to use the data to build statistical models of contractual risk (even if the potential impact is large, likelihood tends to 0). I believe the absence of data, like the dog that didn't bark in the Sherlock Holmes' story, is telling. The usual estimates that

when one-sided terms are put in place, driving defensive behaviour by the weaker side that destroys value. We have also seen high-profile examples where onerous terms failed to guarantee delivery (for example, the famous £10 billion disaster with the National Health Service's IT contracts in the early 2000s).[45]

A final point, if you still need persuading: environmental, social, and governance (ESG) issues are firmly and permanently on the corporate board agenda. How a company interacts with its suppliers, customers, and partners is part of the social aspect of ESG. Unreasonable-going-on-abusive terms and behaviours often used by dominant parties raise real ESG issues and are probably at odds with what their boards claim to care about.

---

are bandied around is that far fewer than 1% of deals end up in material disputes. If this doesn't land for you, consider how likely it is that an issue arises where you would be protected with an unreasonable position, but not with a reasonable position (which, by definition, seeks to address both parties' legitimate concerns). Then consider the cost of winning that position compared to the value of having your contracts start faster. My experience is that we are almost always surprised by what topics come up in disputes (they would have been fully locked down if we knew they were going to be an issue in advance). Better to focus on making sure that it is clear what is going to be done each month and going to be paid. Those tend to be the points that matter in practice and that you can address in advance.

[45] https://www.henricodolfing.com/2019/01/case-study-10-billion-it-disaster.html

Case Study: The Negotiation

A large customer wanted to buy a software-as-a-service product from a small supplier. There was significant business value for the customer once it got the product up and running. Although the product was standard and working with many other customers, the customer needed some minor changes that would take one month to complete.

The customer sent its standard terms, which were unreasonable, and the supplier pushed back. Negotiations dragged on for six months, but eventually, the parties reached a compromise and signed the deal. Despite the negotiations, the supplier had taken on liability far above the value of the contract.

The supplier made sure to spell out the customer's dependencies in the contract to manage the risk. The customer treated this as a transaction and under-resourced the team delivering the dependencies. The customer consequently was responsible for the few delivery delays (the supplier carefully managed the change process given the contract's risks). The supplier delivered the changes in two months from the date of signature with no liability. The project was six months late, and the customer lost significant business value.

The customer's lawyers undoubtedly congratulated themselves on having locked the supplier into a robust contract that ensured delivery. Meanwhile, angels wept.

Case Study 2 - The Negotiation

Automated

I have a complicated relationship with technology. I have been fascinated with it since saving up for a computer at 10, I talk about it regularly at conferences, and we are keen creators and users of it at Radiant Law. But I am also sceptical that everything can and should be automated, especially given contracting is about creating relationships between humans. At the same time, there is no glory or value in carrying out manually the simple and repetitive tasks that a computer can do just as well, if not better.

When it comes to automation, I look to Toyota's approach. Rather than automate complicated processes with sophisticated robots, they first make the process as lean as possible and then apply automation when they hit constraints on further improvements[46]. There is now a rich ecosystem of contracting technology, and some of it really does help. I'm going to devote a significant portion of this book to exploring this area and identifying the systems that give you the most bang for your buck, but core to the RADICAL approach is that you start with getting your processes and basics in order before applying automation. Once you've done that, automate the parts that you sensibly can, while maintaining flexibility.

Data-driven

The contracting world is not short of opinions. As a young lawyer, a long list of rules was beaten into me about what matters and what to do. It's not that these rules are necessarily incorrect, but on reflection, many are arbitrary and few, if any, are informed by data. Firmly held convictions are not the same as objective truth.

If we are going to make progress, we need to measure things that matter and put our beliefs to the test. We need to experiment and be prepared to fail. Almost five hundred years after the start of the scientific revolution, it is time that we embrace empiricism and move beyond handed-down folklore.

Data can be quick and easy to collect, can tell us whether the adjustments we are making are helping, and can be a powerful way to change behaviours. After all, there is nothing quite as compelling

[46] Which doesn't mean that Toyota builds new factories with no automation. There are known solutions that work. They do, however, have a bias towards technology that can be repurposed as they learn.

as numbers. It's time to ditch the fairy tales and find out what works.

Iterative improvements

We've established that there are no silver bullets, but our approach goes further: to avoid transformations as much as possible. Improving contracting is a grind. You need to keep tweaking and learning, and you want to do this as quickly and safely as possible. Try to use small steps with tight feedback loops that are achievable in days or, even better, a few hours. We try to avoid projects that take more than a couple of weeks to deliver as they are probably being over-engineered. You can implement most of the individual actions suggested in this book in that time frame.

Let go of your inner perfectionist for the first version! Try to adopt an approach of getting something—anything—going and improving it from there. Until you use something in practice, it is adding no value. Only when you use it will you understand what works and what doesn't. Pursue perfection in your processes[47] but recognise that you will never achieve it. There is always ***something*** you can improve.

Avoiding a big-bang approach to change is generally a good thing: small changes are easier to get going, lower risk, are more agile, and let you deliver value faster. You may still need transformation projects, but you can make even these relatively small, lightweight, and quick, and it doesn't mean you should make the changes randomly. There is an inherent logic in the sequence, which I describe in this book[48].

---

[47] Perfection is the goal (that is, of course, never reached) of process improvement, but this is not the same as lawyer perfectionism, which can, for example, result in rounds and rounds of drafting tweaks that add little value.

Collaborative

I talked about the need to connect the departments within your organisation and the overall goal of great commercial relationships with the other parties. Collaboration[49] is core to our approach.

Playing nicely within your organisation is obvious; playing nicely with the other side, less so. As I argued with the first principle (contracting should create great relationships), the overall

[48] As noted by one commenter on this book, Lean can involve radical changes as well as ongoing iterative changes, and there is a tension between me arguing for a RADICAL change while espousing iterative changes. Both fair points. My perspective is that there needs to be a transformational change in the mindset around contracting, but teams should err on the side of small, quick changes in implementation, as large IT transformation projects, in particular, have so often had a poor pay-off. Although people don't like discussing failures publicly (we have heard plenty of horror stories off the record), there's a clue in all the articles on the internet about how to avoid the mistakes of the past with contract lifecycle management and how it will be different this time. For more on radical change in Lean, see: http://leanmagazine.net/agile/kaikaku-mind-the-concept-of-radical-change/

[49] Professor Ian Macneil, a founder of the relational approach to contract law, considered cooperation to be at the heart of all relational agreements (and argued that the vast majority of contracts have a relationship component and are not just transactional): "The word 'solidarity' (or 'trust') is not inappropriate to describe this web of interdependence, externally reinforced as well as self-supporting, and expected future co-operation. The most important aspect of solidarity … is the extent to which it produces similarity of selfish interests, whereby what increases (decreases) the utility of one participant also increases (decreases) the utility of the other … Seldom, if ever, is this merger of interests complete, but it is omnipresent, immensely significant, and, in a vast range of circumstances, complete for most practical purposes … [S]imilarity of interests may be produced by external forces such as sovereign law. But … solidarity may and does arise internally in relations." – Economic Analysis of Contractual Relations: Its Shortfalls and the Need for a "Rich Classificatory Apparatus", 75 Northwestern University Law Review 1034.

experience we create for the other side is intrinsic to building confidence and trust and maximising opportunities to generate value. Therefore, the other side is a crucial stakeholder in your process, and the way you engage with them is critical to success.

Accelerated

Speed in contracting is achievable, and nothing is inevitable about the ponderous pace of traditional contracting. I gave you an example in the case study in Chapter 1, where one company was seven times faster than another in closing its contracts. In Chapter 8, I will show you how you can knock 85% off the typical time to close a deal.

My point with putting "accelerated" at the heart of the RADICAL approach is the importance of reducing time to close[50]. Don't worry, even with vastly faster contracting, you still have time to explore options and think through the consequences. Those are things worth spending time on. It's many of the activities that generally soak up time that can be cut back.

Long-term relationships

The objective of your contracting process should be to err on the side of creating long-term rather than transactional relationships. However much we speed up contracting, it will still cost money. If you invest in the relationship, you will be incurring more costs; if you don't, you will be reducing potential value. It's too expensive and wasteful to churn through customers and suppliers, so long-term relationships are valuable[51].

---

[50] There are also times when a speedy contracting process is not in your interest, and you can always slow those deals down. The point is to have the option.

[51] There are also times when transactional is good enough and maximalist

Having a long-term goal means you won't know exactly how it will end up at the point you sign. Therefore, you need to create enough confidence through contracting to let the relationship get going and create enough structure to help you keep growing that relationship. So, flexible contracting arrangements and investment in contract performance management are essential. It also means that win-win is more than a nice-to-have.

> **Case Study: Relationships First**
>
> An in-house lawyer reviewed the contractual disputes at their company to see what changed after the company created its internal legal team and started legal reviews of contracts. They couldn't find any change to the already low number of disputes.
>
> They concluded that the company's long-running focus on building relationships with counterparties was more important than legal reviews.

Case Study 3 - Relationships First

The 3Rs methodology

If you want your contracting to be RADICAL, the obvious questions are: how do we deliver it, and what should come first? This takes us to the 3Rs methodology for implementing RADICAL contracting: Repeatable, Robots, and Refinement.

---

positioning might be the right move. Again, the point is to have the option and to err towards building relationships.

Figure 3 – Repeatable, Robots, Refinement

Underpinning the 3Rs methodology is a crucial observation: contracting is well understood, and you can follow a path that others have created as everyone needs the same essential components. In other words, there is a logical sequence to the changes you want to put in place:

Repeatable: First, put in place the basic tools that can be improved over time, such as contract templates, playbooks, and standard processes. These don't require any automation; in fact, they need to exist before you can start to apply technology.

Robots: Once you have the basics in place, you can introduce technology—in particular, simple technology that includes, where possible, systems already in use within your company. The technology may not end up being the final system but look for quick wins that mean you can get immediate benefits and set yourself up for a continuous improvements approach.

Refinement: Once you have the foundations, you can implement a continuous improvement process driven by stakeholder needs and draw on diverse disciplines, such as Lean, design, and data analytics. In this stage, you will keep getting better, but you will never be done. Perfection will remain elusive, but you'll be able to demonstrate business value, and quality and cost-effectiveness can keep improving at the speed the business needs.

Summary

To fix contracting, we need to think differently. In this chapter, I highlighted the importance of contracts in creating commercial relationships, how you must standardise your processes to improve them, how there are no silver bullets that will fix everything, and the need and opportunity for leadership. Building on these, I introduced the RADICAL approach to contracting: **R**easonable terms, **A**utomated, **D**ata-driven, **I**ncremental improvements, **C**ollaborative, and **A**ccelerated to create **L**ong-term relationships.

We are now going to dive into the 3Rs methodology: Repeatable, Robots, and Refinement that I introduced in chapter 2. In the following six chapters, I will look at each stage, with an introductory chapter on fundamental principles and a subsequent chapter talking through the core improvement activities. I will describe these improvement activities using a pattern (problem, solution, and points to consider) that echoes the pattern language invented by the architect Christopher Alexander[52] and adopted by the software world. There is so much we can learn from outside law!

---

[52] See the book A Pattern Language: Towns, Buildings, Construction by Christopher Alexander.

Chapter 3 Repeatable: Core Principles

The Repeatable stage is about getting the basics in place before thinking about automation. In this chapter, I'm going to cover the fundamental principles that will underpin these basics:

- a framework for the different stages in the contracting process,
- a model for knowledge work,
- how to make knowledge explicit so that everyone in the team can benefit,
- how to approach implementing change in a way that sticks,
- the behaviour in your team that you will want to encourage,
- how to move past heroics, and
- the implications of whether you start with your template.

The contracting process

"***All models are wrong, but some are useful.***" - George Box

At the heart of the Repeatable stage is the principle that we can standardise contracting and have a consistent process for handling contracts of a particular type.

I am going to be following a generic set of high-level stages for the contracting process.

Figure 4 - Stages of a deal

- **Initiate:** This covers the start of the deal when the basic principles are being agreed. In sales, this would run from leads through to an almost-closed opportunity. In procurement, this would include needs recognition and early stages, such as requests for information and proposals. When the procurement process involves competition, that will also fall into the drafting and negotiation stages. From the contracting team's perspective, "initiate" covers the intake process when the team is engaged for assistance and starts collecting information on what is needed.

- **Draft:** This covers the creation of the first draft of the contract. Although there will be ongoing drafting as part of the negotiation of the contract terms, I have made generating the first draft a distinct stage because much of the legal tech for drafting treats the process as a one-off event (afterwards, it usually becomes redline in Word).

- **Negotiate:** This covers the in-depth negotiations of the contract. Although it appears after drafting, there will often have been at least commercial-level discussions before the drafting stage. If the other side created the first draft of the contract, this stage would also include your review of that draft.

- **Sign:** This covers signing the actual agreement and the approvals process.

- **Manage:** Once the contract is signed, the relationship needs to be maintained. This stage covers the hand-over and operationalising of the agreement and the contractual relationship management, including future changes and extensions and any eventual termination.

There are a couple of things to bear in mind about this model. First, it's pretty legal-centric and errs towards higher volume contracting. Procurement might describe the drafting and negotiation stages as just one step in their model of the process. Sales would probably mutter something about "papering the deal". These are fair points, but I have split the process up like this because:

- it enables us to reason about both sales and procurement contracting processes at the same time,
- it helps make sense of the legal tech market, and
- these are the main steps for turning a vague consensus into a legally enforceable contract.

Second, much of the value from the commercial relationship is created in the initiation and management steps. It's how you select your partners, nurture the relationship, and create value for one another that will drive success. The contracting process can add clarity, increase trust, and give you the confidence to get going, but it's just part of a bigger picture. And that's the heart of the RADICAL approach: we need contracts, but it's not all about the contracts.

Contracting as knowledge work

"***The most important contribution management needs to make in the 21st century is similarly to increase the productivity of knowledge work and the knowledge worker***" - Peter Drucker

I discussed in Chapter 2 how the contracting process needs to be standardised, this is also true about contracting knowledge.

Contracting is knowledge work, but not all knowledge work is the same. Imagine a spectrum for knowledge work, ranging between routine work at one end and innovative work at the other[53]. With routine work, knowledge is explicit, scenarios are predictable, and the work may be complicated but it is not complex[54]. With innovative work, knowledge is often tacit[55], scenarios are novel, and the problems are often complex as well as complicated.

If you ask people to choose where a particular piece of contracting work fits on the routine-innovation spectrum and explain their thinking, you will likely observe a range of answers informed by two factors. First, how often the person has done the work before. If it's a common deal for them (or their organisation), they will tend to describe it as more routine; if they haven't seen it before, the work will likely be considered more innovative. Second, the incentives in play. If the person is motivated for the work to be considered novel, complex and requiring expertise, they will tend to position it as innovative. If they are motivated for the work to be simple, they

---

[53] Autor, Levy, and Murnane made a similar distinction between routine and non-routine tasks in their 2003 paper The Skill Content of Recent Technological Change: An Empirical Exploration.

[54] Complicated systems and tasks may have many interconnected parts, but how the parts interact is predictable. Complex systems and tasks have emergent properties from how the parts interact, which are not necessarily predictable from understanding the individual parts.

[55] Tacit knowledge is personal, experiential, and hard (but not necessarily impossible) to articulate or document. Tacit knowledge is what we associate with experts, but at least some tacit knowledge can be codified to become explicit knowledge.

will tend to position it as routine. As I observed in Chapter 1, incentives matter.

You can break the work down further. A deal may be generally routine, but have a few uncommon points. Perhaps those uncommon points are novel and need fresh thinking. Perhaps the person doing the deal has decades of experience and seen them before. Experienced lawyers have just seen a wider range of issues and have had more opportunities to try different approaches. So, whether work is deemed to be routine or innovative can be quite subjective.

Treating the work as innovative implies a wide range of outcomes, but there is huge value in reliably and consistently dealing with issues in your contracts:

- you need to address the issues that matter every time, and some outcomes will be better that others,
- you will want to be able to reason about your contracts as a portfolio when you have to address future changes such as a new law or an acquisition,
- your organisation needs to deliver what has been promised, and novel requirements in contracts will introduce operational headaches,
- improving your contract content over time, like improving your contract process, needs a written standard that can be improved, and
- making tacit knowledge explicit allows everyone to learn together, improving how well everyone does their jobs, including experienced lawyers.

So we want contracting content and issue handling to become more routine over time, while retaining the capability to handle novel deals and issues thoughtfully[56].

This model has implications:

- Experienced lawyers should be focusing on deals and other areas where there is novelty and ambiguity. These scenarios tend to have higher value, risk, complexity, and ambiguity. Junior lawyers should be given the tools and codified knowledge they need to handle routine work. Experienced lawyers doing the same routine deals every day is a waste for the organisation, and unsatisfying for the lawyer. Still, it is valuable for experienced team members to provide judgement calls on novel points that come up in routine deals.

- Experienced lawyers should also be simplifying templates, codifying knowledge, and building standards.

- Your organisation may be treating deals as innovative work that external providers, who support thousands of deals for many different clients, may see as routine. These providers can tell you what is the market standard and bring codified knowledge in templates and playbooks to accelerate making your deals more routine.

---

[56] There is a useful model in the Lean world for classifying work as either runners, repeaters, or strangers. Runners are deals that happen every day, repeaters come in with regularity but less often, and strangers are rarities. Focusing your improvement efforts on runners, including making their handling more routine, will yield the most benefits. Using more experienced lawyers to handle strangers will be the best immediate tactic (although more junior lawyers can learn a lot from trying new things).

- A deal is not inherently complex just because it has some regulatory, industry, or organisation-specific issues. These types of issues can be codified remarkably quickly, and experience can translate across deal types.

The point is not to remove innovative work from jobs. I believe that too much contracting work is treated as innovative when it could be made more routine, meaning it could be done by more people and be more susceptible to automation. The goal, however, is to free up time that can be spent being genuinely innovative to create more value for your organisation. There is no limit to the value that can be created, but there is a limit to available resources.

Knowledge management

"***If HP knew what HP knows, we'd be three times more productive.***" – Former Hewlett-Packard CEO, Lew Platt

At the heart of what you are doing in the Repeatable stage is moving your contracting process from individual opinions applied in an ad-hoc way to a shared, explicit method. As described in the previous section, this is core work for the experienced members in your team; and can be helped by external providers who bring the codified knowledge, as well as processes, needed to make contracting both routine and repeatable.

Examples of explicit knowledge are templates, clause databases, playbooks, training materials, checklists, and process maps, which we will cover in the next chapter.

As you do this, consider the following:

- **Making knowledge explicit can be threatening**: If people in your team feel that their value depends on the knowledge in their head, they will be reluctant to share. Early in the exercise, focus on incentives and make sure that your team understands the importance—for both the organisation and for them personally—of moving to a more systematised approach, including the opportunity for more exciting work.

- **There is a trade-off between action and control**: The more controls you put in place around who can make changes to your playbooks and templates, the slower you'll move and the less participation you'll get in suggesting modifications. It's all too easy to kill continuous improvement in practice, so I urge you to take a liberal approach and allow team members to make changes. The reality is that it's better to get less-than-perfect contractual approaches documented, explicit, and capable of being improved than for sub-optimal hidden practices to continue.

- **Avoid creating too many documents**: Documents are excellent places to hide knowledge. They act like coffins (and document management systems act like graveyards). Try to keep this explicit knowledge in as few places as possible and err on the side of storing it in wiki pages (i.e., your own private Wikipedia) rather than documents.

- **Consistency across regions**: Multi-national organisations will have challenges with adopting a consistent approach, so start with the larger centres and see if you can find ways to highlight local exceptions rather than accept completely different methods.

- **Gravitate towards more structure**: There is a continuum of how structured your knowledge is, with entirely free-form documents at one end and databases at the other. Different types of knowledge can sit in various places along that spectrum. However, try to move towards more structure. If in doubt, try to use a table rather than an essay to document positions and hold clauses in databases rather than in old contracts sitting on a shelf in your office.

- **It's not about the technology**: We spend a lot of time refining Radiant Law's systems, but that doesn't mean that technology is the priority. What matters most is building a culture of shared learning.

Finally, making knowledge explicit is about individuals. The reality (which conflicts with what we would like it to be) is that a few people will make a vast contribution and that single-handed Herculean efforts are what makes the difference between a helpful system and one that's ignored. Though we encourage everyone to participate, it's the few who will make all the difference, and it's worth rewarding their efforts, as long as they find a way to bring the team along with them. I will come back to that last point.

Implementing change

"***People don't resist change. They resist being changed!***" – Peter Senge

Tools

During each stage of the 3Rs, you will be implementing new tools and approaches. Therefore, now is the time to consider how best to approach these projects and build your organisational change muscles.

The most critical part of the Repeatable stage is making sure that the contracting team uses the same process and approach and deals become more routine. If this isn't the norm yet in your organisation, it can come as a big shock to the team members.

However, it's an inevitable part of maturing and reflects the necessary mindset of improving together rather than operating as islands. Making a change as an individual is far less valuable than making a change as a team. If you can't spread improvements through the team, they will have little impact and likely die off.

The key to making effective change is avoiding perfectionism, which can be challenging for lawyers! Making something better, getting it used, and then coming back and improving it again later is far more valuable than working on it until it's "perfect"[57].

Similarly, you'll want to adopt the Pareto Principle[58], which says that 80% of the value will come from 20% of the effort. Avoiding completionism, as well as perfectionism, is essential. It's much better to get a simple tool in place to cover at least one common-use case and then extend it once it is being used. That way, you'll have an idea of what matters in practice, which will often be very different from what you might have thought beforehand.

Overall, I urge you to adopt an approach of prioritising action over never-ending discussion and, if in doubt, just do it. There's no need for projects to improve contract templates to take six months. They can be improved in mere weeks and then improved again later.

---

[57] This argument may be counter-intuitive for readers with legal training. We have had it drummed into us that we must get it right, that spending more time will lead to better outcomes, and that we have to avoid being open to being second guessed in the future. Process improvement thinking brings a different perspective: we only know when something will work by identifying a metric and then trying out the "improvement" and seeing whether the metric gets better. For more on applying empiricism to improvement, see these articles on the plan-do-check/study-act cycle (PDCA or PDSA):
https://www.thinkleansixsigma.com/article/pdca-cycle and
https://www.process.st/deming-cycle/

[58] https://www.investopedia.com/terms/p/paretoprinciple.asp

Repeatable: Core Principles

Here are some principles for how to approach implementing change:

- **Momentum:** Starting with small wins and building an ethos of continuous improvement will help set the context in which more ambitious projects can be rolled out.

- **Have a plan and a budget:** You need a plan for rolling out improvements and to make someone (or a small group) accountable for delivery, who are empowered and publicly supported from the top. You need to budget not only for the initial activity or system but also for the implementation and training costs. Implementation costs can be high—in some cases, they're more than the cost of the system itself.

- **Sell the benefits**: You need to sell the benefits, not just to the organisation but also to team members. Communication throughout the project is essential. The basic rule is that you cannot over-communicate.

- **Minimise the pain**: You should select and implement the project in a way that makes the personal process of change as easy as possible. Use pilots and testing, and knock the edges off before rolling it out widely.

- **Champions and beachheads**: Get going with champions first to ensure that you can demonstrate a fully working tool or system before a wider roll-out. Find enthusiasts who look for potential (rather than problems) to be your champions.

- **Training:** Training is usually essential, but it doesn't necessarily have to be done by external providers. Enthusiastic champions are often the best people to train the rest of the team.

- **Finally, pick up the sceptics**: Once the new system or tool is in place and working, you can address the sceptics and do what you need to do to get them using it. Sceptics bring a lot of value, too. They will ask the hard questions and force the rigour that will be needed in the long run.

- **Persistence**: There will be setbacks, and not everyone will leap at the opportunity to use the new system or tool. Keeping at it when you know it does work and will help is essential (keeping at it with a fundamentally flawed system is less helpful). Making it easier to adopt the change rather than continuing on the old path will also be invaluable.

Behaviour

What I've described above are the standard tactics for rolling out new tools; but tools are necessary, not sufficient. RADICAL contracting is at its heart about changing behaviour.

I talked about some ideal behaviours during the contracting process itself in Chapter 2. Here are some more relating to how the contracting team works together and improves how contracting is done:

- Following a documented process that is improved by everyone (standard work in Lean terminology), rather than everyone working in their own way.

- Making knowledge explicit, including in standard playbooks, rather than hoarding it.

- Building continuous improvement habits and investing the time each day in improving the overall contracting process, not just supporting contracts themselves.

- Acting with agency and fixing issues rather than just assuming that things can't be improved.

- Moving to a results-orientated culture, where the team focuses on the outcomes that matter and the behaviour needed to achieve those outcomes.

- Thinking systemically, and considering the impact on other parts of the organisation of decisions that are made.

- Being bold in adopting more reasonable positions, cutting the fluff out of contract templates, and simplifying how the work is done.

None of these are easy or comfortable to adopt. This is probably exacerbated by lawyers, as a cohort, being more cats than dogs. They are generally smart and excellent at abstract reasoning, but they also are also highly sceptical and autonomous, while low in resilience and sociability[59]. I have heard many general counsel and law firm leaders despair at changing how their team behaves.

One response to this has been to focus on the tools in the hope that this will somehow lead to different behaviour. It sounds ridiculous when put this way, but I regularly see projects (especially CLM projects, which I will come to later) that appear to have an underpinning assumption that if only the team would save their documents in a particular place, or use a workflow tool to coordinate with others, then the team would cooperate and work

[59] From an analysis by Dr. Larry Richard, who found that lawyers were two standard deviations above the norm in scepticism (93rd percentile) and autonomy (89th percentile), two standard deviations below the norm in sociability (even with rainmakers, they were in the 12th percentile) and one standard deviation below the norm in resilience (30th percentile).

effectively. Pushing new buttons is not the behavioural change I'm describing in this book.

It may give you hope that the Radiant Law team, consisting predominantly of lawyers who have all the characteristics described above, are a long way down this change path. We got there by being strict about the need for a single way of working and ongoing improvement, but pushing the decisions on how the work is done and what to improve next, to the people doing the work[60].

So it's possible and we don't need to accept the findings about the typical lawyer as the end of the conversation. As one observer suggested to me, lawyers may be sceptical and hard to initially change, but if you can get over the “hump” of motivation and scepticism, their brilliant brains can help them get to the answer faster, and cut through the noise to see the points that matter. There is likely a lot of mental fire power lurking in your team.

Achieving behavioural change requires time and consistency. The value that change brings also tends to be more important with routine than innovative work, where there is greater variability and need for creativity in the deal itself. This is why many of Radiant Law's clients have outsourced their higher volume contracts to us, allowing their team to focus on the more complex and strategic deals, and I discuss this approach in chapter 9.

The importance of behaviour over just new tools is also why Radiant Law has gotten out of the business of helping with templates or tools as standalone projects. Without the necessary

---

[60] "You can’t think your way into right action, but you act your way to right thinking", as Bill Wilson observed. We insist that the Radiant Law team experiments and tries at least something. The experience the team members then have does seem to change their beliefs about what is possible and their subsequent behaviour.

accompanying behavioural changes, we didn't feel we were adding enough value with these projects, and indeed there have been times when it seemed we were just there to tick the innovation box for the legal team's annual goals. We now only provide full solutions for clients, supporting categories of contracts and delivering the full outcome our clients need, while the internal team focuses on strategic deals. Everyone is a winner if we can be honest about the art of the possible.

Collaboration, heroics, and mentors

"It is amazing what you can accomplish if you do not care who gets the credit." - Harry S. Truman

"Collaborative" is part of RADICAL contracting and the fourth principle was "fixing contracting requires leadership and a team". Let's explore further how individuals and departments might work with others within your organisation.

I see a lot of heroic behaviour in contracting; I have also seen heroics lead to burn-out. At the same time, I see many legal departments concerned about how they are perceived and valued by the "business" and Professor Laura Empson has described many lawyers as being "insecure overachievers". I fear there is a destructive pattern at play of a need to be seen leading to poor outcomes for organisations and team members.

I'm going to discuss in the next chapter how the intake process needs to change to balance the load, but there are broader points to explore about where we seek satisfaction in our work and how we choose to influence, and collaborate with, others.

A pair of economists once analysed different sports as weak-link versus strong-link games[61]. In weak-link games, the team is as strong as the weakest player (they gave football as an example), in strong-link games, the team is as strong as the strongest player (e.g., basketball). My sense is that contracting is a weak-link game. It is rare that one person can see the whole of the deal, different parts are often lead by different departments, and there are many ways that contracts can fail to achieve their purpose. Going further, the relationship created by the contract needs both parties to play their part if it is to succeed.

This suggests that heroics on deals not only won't save the day, but may be counter-productive, not only for the health of the individual involved but also in inadvertently discouraging others from pulling their weight.

I suspect that how the broader contracting process performs is also a weak-link game, as is improving the contracting process; but we need to be careful when it comes to improvements. I have seen individuals make outsized contributions, and I discussed that in the knowledge management section above, but those contributions will only add value if the broader team adopts the improvement. It is not enough for someone to create a new resource or tool, it is incumbent on them to share, teach, encourage, cajole, and do whatever else is needed to get to broader adoption. Otherwise, what's the point?

There is another aspect to heroics: influencing others by choosing to take the role of the mentor, not the hero. There is a well known archetypal story called the Hero's Journey (also known as the monomyth as it is a pattern that appears so often in stories). Joseph Campbell described it as "A hero ventures forth from the world of

---

[61] The Numbers Game: Why Everything You Know about Soccer is Wrong by Chris Anderson and David Sully, later popularised by a Malcolm Gladwell podcast.

common day into a region of supernatural wonder: fabulous forces are there encountered and a decisive victory is won: the hero comes back from this mysterious adventure with the power to bestow boons on his fellow man." One of the key elements of the story is the role of the mentor: a person who helps and guides the hero on their journey.

From the perspective of the deal, I have emphasised the importance of relationships, and how relationships are ultimately between individuals. Contracting underpins the formation of the relationship, but who at your organisation will take the relationship forwards after signing? Should the representative of the contracts team lead the creation of the relationship with the team at the other party, or is their role best seen as the mentor to the business representative who will carry on the day-to-day relationship?

Similarly, with improvement projects. Given the cross-departmental nature of contracting, is the contracts team going to get the broadest impact by being seen to own the project, at the risk of being ignored by others? Or will it have greater influence by helping other departments, even if it means that it isn't seen as the hero of the story?

People still need to have their contributions recognised. The question I am posing is: what behaviour should leaders praise?

Whose paper?

"Every decision that you take maintains the status quo, reverses your steps or hastens your steps" - DJ Bwakali

One last topic before turning to the individual steps to put a Repeatable process in place: the importance of which party's terms are used at the start of the contract process. There's a massive advantage in your paper[62] being the starting point of a negotiation:

- there are only so many points that the other side can raise in practice, and it gives you a boost out of the gate on smaller topics[63],
- it significantly reduces the effort involved in the negotiation stage (you know your way around your template), and
- you can set the tone for the subsequent negotiations.

Given that there is so much value in using your paper, prioritise producing strong templates to use in common deals. You're creating far more work for yourself if you keep using the other side's drafts rather than creating your own template. However, unless it's completely relevant, insisting on your paper for a specialist deal is unhelpful. You may have all the negotiating leverage in the world, but a software licence is not going to be remotely appropriate for a software-as-a-service deal. Your ability to always use your templates will also vary depending on leverage and conventions. Still, it's a lot easier to persuade the other side to use your paper if it's short, clear, reasonable, and relevant, which we'll explore further in the next chapter.

The consequences of working from the other side's paper are:

- You'll use a more general and principle-led playbook, but that will probably only exist if you do a lot of those deals,

---

[62] "Your paper" means that the first draft of the contract was created by you—hopefully using a template.

[63] "Reasonable" terms cover a range of possible outcomes. If a provision is good enough for the other side, they will usually accept the clause even if it's not optimal. This creates an opportunity to fine tune your terms, avoiding lengthy negotiations while obtaining good outcomes.

and if you do, are you sure you can't move them to your paper?

- You may well go straight to a "red flag" risk analysis and then to signature if you have only a low degree of negotiation leverage for the deal.

There are also now new standard terms available in commercial contracting. This is an old phenomenon in other sectors such as finance, trade, and construction[64], but now OneNDA, Bonterms, and the WorldCC standard clauses have appeared, offering middle-of-the-road solutions for common contract types. There are even terms addressing climate change produced by the excellent Chancery Lane Project. As these get increasingly adopted, both parties will be more likely to be familiar with the terms which should speed up discussions. Adopting them is also a powerful signal that your company is reasonable and focused on the relationship rather than optimising legal positions. Have a look and see if you can make them work for your needs.

Summary

This chapter looked at some of the fundamental underpinning principles that will apply in the Repeatable stage and beyond. I set out a generic structure for thinking about your contracting: initiation, drafting, negotiation, signing, and management. I discussed a model for routine v innovative knowledge work, and the value in making contracting more routine over time by making knowledge explicit. This requires taking knowledge management seriously, and I gave some pointers on how to approach this. I covered how to implement tools, with a strong emphasis on quick

[64] Examples include the ISDA and LMA terms in finance, INCOTERMS definitions in trade, and the FIDIC, NEC, and AIA terms for construction.

projects rather than transformational change. I then looked at the, arguably most important, challenge of changing behaviour which takes time, and the role of heroics. Finally, I discussed the implications of whether or not you use your templates.

Now that we've covered the basics, let's look at the problems in the Repeatable stage and the solutions you can apply. Getting these fundamentals in place will put your contracting process on the right footing to start using technology.

Chapter 4 Repeatable: The Steps

It's now time to learn how to implement the Repeatable stage principles. Here are the tools and processes to put in place in the Repeatable stage (I've added a "Track" column for managing your contracting process).

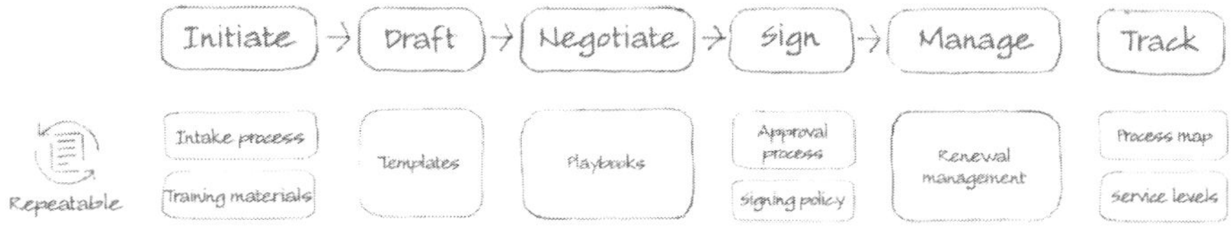

Figure 7 - Repeatable stage steps

These are the core building blocks for a successful process, but don't worry about perfection at this point. You just want to get something in place that can be used and then improved.

Intake and service levels

The problem

How best to enable business users to request help with their contracts?

The solution

- Create a form for starting the process so that the necessary information can be collected the first time, improving consistency and avoiding going back and forth. Consider giving the business team the ability to create simple contracts themselves.

- Create a process that enables requests to be sent to a single place so that the contracting team can triage them and decide who should support them. There may be different places to go in large organisations for particular contracts (e.g., procurement v sales).

- Define target service levels for acknowledging and completing responses, so the initiator has some predictability and can plan accordingly.

- The contracting team could set minimum thresholds to avoid needing to be involved in low-risk contracts (covered in the next section).

Points to consider

At some point, someone in the business is going to need assistance with a contract. They will need somewhere to send their request and will undoubtedly appreciate a prompt response in a predictable timeframe.

Too often, this critical stage is ill-defined. The initiator asks the person who helped them last time, there's some to-ing and fro-ing with questions, and finally, something happens. This approach, while common, is neither good for the contracts team nor the business. Contract team members may like to be liked, but high performance is rewarded with too many requests and over-work. It's not sustainable. An unstructured approach also means that time and effort is spent gathering the needed information—it's slow and inefficient for everyone involved.

The better approach is a formal intake process with a central place to ask for help and a structured form to collect relevant information. No one likes completing forms but gathering this information avoids going back and forth every time; the questions, of course, should be kept to an absolute minimum[65]. I'm going to cover how to create great forms in Chapter 5.

Not being able to go to their favourite helper also won't appeal to the business. Still, clear service levels for responding and completing the activity are the quid pro quo for the intake process change. In the Refinement stage, you're going to measure and improve the actual performance against the service levels, but this would be a great time to start to keep track[66].

Identifying risks

Problem

How can you make sure that risks in your contracts are being checked and approved by the right people?

Solution

We will be covering a more comprehensive approach to contract risk management in Chapter 8. For now, put in place:

- a risk-based triage as part of the intake process to confirm who is best placed to handle the agreement (which may be the business),

---

[65] You may encounter "evaders"—individuals who try to avoid the process, only complete parts of the form, or otherwise don't play nice. How you respond will depend on the culture of your company, but it's better to handle this head on. For example, you might enforce field completion on the form, require additional training for repeat offenders, or provide data back to managers on performance.

[66] You will likely want to know how many requests are coming in, where they came from, and what type of help is needed. We sometimes see teams measuring their workload using open matters. I suggest you use new matters instead; otherwise it encourages letting deals drag on and doesn't give you a good sense of capacity (open matters may not even be touched in any particular month).

- an approval process so that relevant departments and managers sign off on their part of the agreement and any identified material risks, and

- a signing policy to make sure that an appropriate person signs the contract. The management level required should depend on the risks involved.

Points to consider

Not all contracts are created equal. Some require proper vetting and attention, while others only need the basics checked. Send agreements to the appropriate support, approvers, and signer with a thoughtful process.

Fears about risk have led to the overuse of legal resources, with contracting teams becoming bogged down in reviewing contracts that are probably never going to be significant causes of trouble. You inevitably have limited resources and want to direct them appropriately, so head off low-risk contracts at the initiation stage and free up the contracting team to work on more critical agreements.

The following are typical indicators of whether particular attention is required:

- the value and committed term of the transaction,

- if the contract uses an unmodified standard form,

- if it is just renewing an existing approved deal,

- any material security or reputational risks,

- any granting of guarantees or security,

- any processing of personal data, and
- any material IP being created or transferred.

Some teams specify cut-off rules when they don't need to be involved, such as "less than £X in value, unless they touch on risk areas A, B or C". Others use a points system to determine how risky a contract is. Either way, a stratification of risk is a helpful way to triage work.

Business self-help

Problem

The contracting team doesn't have enough time to support every contract. How can more of the contract drafting process be devolved to the business to help themselves?

Solution

Part of the solution will come at the Robots stage, but there are basics that you can put in place now to help the business do more:

- content that explains unintuitive points to the other side early in the process to head off misunderstandings,
- a playbook and training materials on the issues that you want the business team to cover early on in discussions with the other side,
- user-friendly and straightforward template agreements for use by the business team (these will be automated in the Robots stage), and

- a training programme to make sure that the basics are well understood by the business team.

You should also establish one place for the business team to access these resources, and we'll cover that in the Robots stage.

Points to consider

Getting the business team to the point where they can support themselves with more straightforward contracts and do more work in the early stages of more complex transactions is attractive. Still, you need to take the following into account:

- it needs to be done safely,
- everyone has plenty to do already, so if you're just passing work to the next-door department, it will likely take them as least as long as it does your department and won't be helping the organisation, and
- you need to simplify tasks you're giving to people with less training.

Standard templates

Problem

How do you get more deals onto your paper and reduce the amount of time spent on multiple rounds of negotiations?

Solution

Create a suite of modular standard templates for the most common deal types that are short, clear, reasonable, and relevant.

Points to consider

As noted in the previous chapter, using your templates at the start of the deal offers many advantages. That will be more likely if your templates not only exist but are also fit for purpose and easy to digest by the other side. I argued that terms should be more reasonable, going straight to the middle ground. Your goal should also be short, clear, reasonable, and relevant terms. I discussed reasonableness in Chapter 2, but let's consider the other dimensions.

The **length**, it turns out, is particularly relevant. It has a dramatic effect on first impressions, and an agreement of only a few pages is far more likely to be looked at quickly and accepted.

Case Study: Shorter Terms

As an example of shortening terms, we took one client's contract and reduced it from about fourteen pages to three.

We didn't lose any of the material points in the agreement through this reduction, which illustrates how unnecessarily verbose typical legal language is.

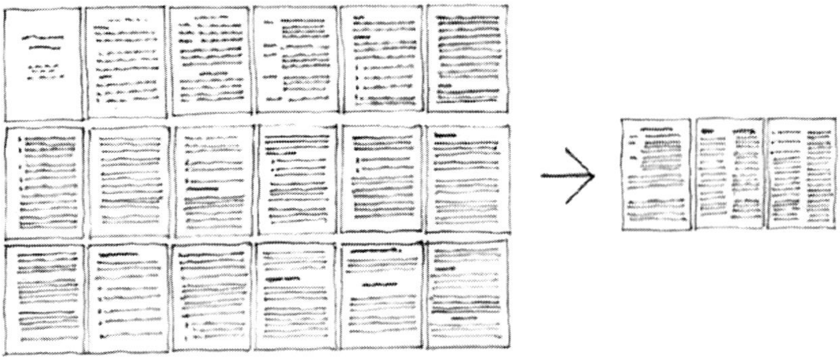

Figure 8 - Simplifying a Contract

As part of this exercise, we also changed a few unreasonable provisions to some that were more mainstream but still addressed the client's real concerns. We moved the agreement's specifics up front, making the commercial details the focus of the document.

The result was we reduced the average time to signature from months to just days, with fewer than 10 per cent of the agreements requiring negotiation. The reasonableness of the terms, not just the length, was also critical to the result.

Case Study 4 - Shorter Terms

As you shorten and simplify your agreements (if no one can remember why a provision was included, this might be an excellent time to get rid of it), you'll also want to **clarify** the language.

The drive towards clear contracts is part of the Plain English movement, but clear contracts are still contracts. The language of contracting is inevitably somewhat technical because we want contracts to be rigorous and enforceable, as well as usable. There is less tolerance for ambiguity and inconsistency of terminology than is acceptable with other written works.

Halfway between code and prose, contracts need special rules, and I commend to you ***A Manual of Style for Contract Drafting*** by Ken Adams as the go-to text on how to phrase your contracts. As a keen advocate of removing words, using thought-through terminology, and careful handling of potential ambiguities, Ken brings to contracts a rigour that is much needed to challenge the passed-down habits that have characterised much thinking in this area to date. Ken's work also lifts the lid on how awful most contract drafting is[67].

In addition to clarifying the language, look at how you structure your contract. Try to design it to make it more accessible and more acceptable to the other side. Consider the order and structure (key terms up front, legal issues afterwards, and the particularly dull topics right at the back) and make it data-oriented (separating the data points or otherwise making them easy to extract[68]).

---

[67] There is also a new ISO standard for plain language, which I recommend reading: ISO 24495-1:2023

[68] See, for example, content controls in Word https://learn.microsoft.com/en-us/office/vba/word/concepts/working-with-word/working-with-content-controls

Finally, your terms need to be **relevant** and focused on the essential provisions for the deal. They should not include "just in case" provisions (helping with length, too). Make your terms modular and maintain a separate library (which can be a shared document in the first iteration) of clauses relevant in less common circumstances. This will be a lot easier to manage once you've implemented the document automation described in the Robots section.

There will be a trade-off between relevance and the frequency with which you handle a deal of a particular type. It's not worth having templates for the less common agreements and trying to impose overly generic terms will often slow a deal down rather than speed it up. There are times when accepting the use of the other side's terms with dignity is a virtue.

Despite this, err on the side of having your own good templates:

- Producing an initial draft from a contract template is significantly faster than working from old deals.

- Good templates help ensure that your team considers the relevant issues, lead to better drafting, and make the final contract more consistent and predictable (greatly enhancing your ability to manage the contract).

- Templates are the foundation for further development, forming the basis for several additional stages of improving your contracting processes, including document automation and playbooks.

- With a consistent set of agreements, it is easier to update them as laws change, review them to identify variations in positions taken, or extract key data points.

Generally, templates have a leveraging effect. If they're good, you'll see the impact across your contracting process—likewise, if they're bad. Consistency through standard terms is better than inconsistency (unless you consistently send out agreements with the same error in them). The upshot is that time invested in improving your contract templates more than pays for itself.

One final thought. People generally consider themselves to be reasonable; the authors of contract templates tend to be proud of their work. Yet when I ask people how often they receive short, clear, reasonable, and relevant contracts from the other side, they say rarely. May I gently suggest that you ask others for their opinion of your templates before you assume that you have nailed it.

Playbooks

Problem

How do you improve the consistency of negotiations and control risk during the negotiation phase?

Solution

Create a playbook for each standard template and any other common agreements that you review on the other side's paper, along with a process for updating them. Appoint one or more owners to approve inclusions and proactively update the playbooks.

Points to consider

By creating standard terms, you effectively crystallise your preferred positions on the different topics that come up within a given type of agreement. What this doesn't help with is:

- when the other side raises issues with your draft, or

- when you're working with the other side's first draft.

Traditionally, the answer is to make it up as you go along, depending on the reviewer involved and what their mood is. This makes the expertise in your team hard to share and the negotiation process even harder to standardise.

The solution is a playbook. It's a document that captures what to do when you see an issue that regularly comes up in a negotiation. There are effectively two types of playbooks:

- **The other side's paper**: When reviewing the other side's paper, the playbook is likely to be a list of points based on principle, often structured as points you want to see covered in the agreement and points that you don't want to appear.

- **Your paper**: When it's your agreement, you should structure the playbook by following the underlying template's order (with a few general points up front). You will find it reasonably easy to predict where the other side will raise issues.

Whoever owns it, the playbook should be a structured repository of knowledge and initially[69], at least, presented as a table:

Clause	Issue	Action	Reason

Figure 9 - Playbook structure

[69] At Radiant Law, we've built a knowledge structure in a database that allows us to connect issues across our clients' playbooks, show what is "market", and provide our team with supporting knowledge at the point they need it. Still, we started with Word documents.

If you want to create a discursive explanation of topics and points, keep them in separate documents (or even better, a wiki). Playbooks are practical tools, and every word you add slows the user down, so keep them as tight as possible. Don't seek exhaustive completeness; if you keep adding rows, your playbook will eventually become unusable. Instead, focus on the key issues.

To get going, I suggest you get an experienced member of your team to create a simple starting point, or if you're feeling inclusive, get several team members to identify the most common issues and come up with the standard responses. It would help if you then implemented a rule that every time someone asks for advice on a new material point, they should include the answer in the playbook. Your playbook should be a living document, so you need to have a process in place to ensure it is updated regularly and everyone is using the latest version.

Another challenge you may experience is that it's a lot easier, emotionally, to treat every decision as unique and avoid committing to a standard position. We often see teams being reluctant to decide on an authoritative answer to a particular situation—and then they're surprised that they can't get those contracts off their desks. If a change is exceptional, at least try to define when the exception applies. The rules could refer to, for example, the size of the deal and its strategic importance. There will always be situations where escalations are needed, and you can specify these in the playbook.

One thing to consider is whether you can give playbooks to the business users to help move the early stages of negotiations "upstream". With this use case, you need to keep it extremely simple with clear "if-then" rules and triggers for when to refer to legal. Including more in-depth explanations can be tempting but try to keep it to the point.

Finally, it's often better to get rid of a negotiation point than to capture it in a playbook. When issues come up, consider if you can get rid of them by tweaking your standard terms. Similarly, rather than having multiple fallback steps in your playbook, perhaps you could go straight to the end position to speed up discussions?

Process maps

Problem

How do you turn a stream of emails and documents into a shared understanding of the process?

Solution

Map your processes, share them with the team, and use them as the cornerstone of your future Robot and Refinement stage activities.

Points to consider

The realities of your current contracting processes are probably even more complex, convoluted, and inconsistent than you fear, but that's fixable. The starting point is to understand "as-is" reality, and there's nothing like a picture to make things clear.

Our preferred starting visualisation is a swim lane diagram—a flowchart overlaid onto "swim lanes" representing the different participants. Here's a simplified example:

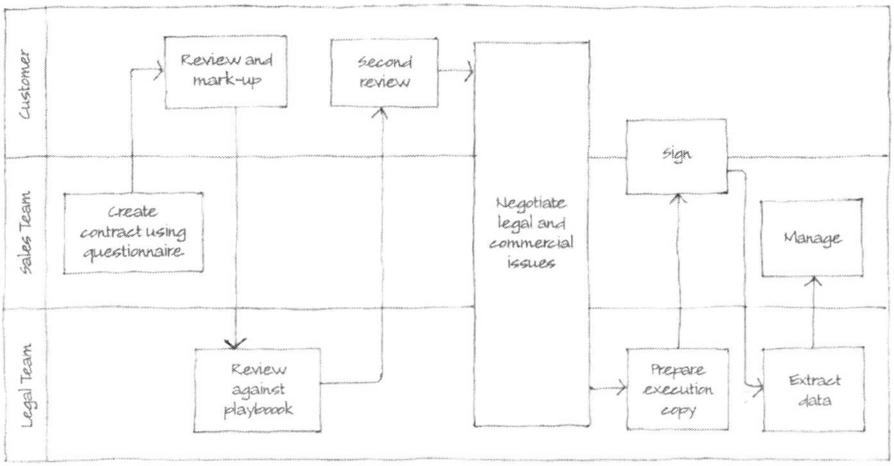

Figure 10 - Swimlane diagram

The easiest way to create one is with a few people who are intimately familiar with the process, a whiteboard, Post-it notes for the steps, and pens for the arrows. Don't worry at the beginning about what the process should look like. Just focus on what happens—the current state. Use different-coloured Post-it notes to represent the value the step delivers in meeting the stakeholders' needs:

- steps that are adding real value,
- steps that are not adding real value but are necessary (at least for now), and
- steps that are not adding value.

Now is also an excellent time to start counting. I talk about data in detail in Chapter 7, but for now, begin to collect data on:

- how many deals you are doing,
- the average time spent working on the deal in each stage,

- the average time a deal stays in each stage, and
- the most common obstacles faced by your team.

The answers will give you an excellent view of the waste and delays in the process[70].

Once you understand what is happening (in as much detail as possible), you can think about the future state. You're pretty much guaranteed to get some quick wins from this process, as once you understand what's going on, you'll spot steps that just don't make sense, are not adding value, and are not necessary. You'll want to keep refining, removing steps where possible, and ensuring that you focus as much effort as possible on the things that add the most value.

We will come back to improvements in the Refinement stage, but for now, enjoy getting a glimpse into the underlying madness of your organisation.

Deal sheets

Problem

How do you keep everyone aligned about what matters and what is happening on a particular deal? [71]

---

[70] You can start to compare, for example, the time that is spent actually doing the work (called the process time) against the time in the stage (the lead time). For a review of a document, it will probably be an hour or two of process time and days or weeks of lead time. Not a great ratio, but common for services at an early stage of development. If you are interested in exploring this area more, see Karen Martin and Mike Osterling's book ***Value Stream Mapping***.

[71] Many thanks to Jeff Carr for introducing me to this approach.

Solution

For your material deals, identify the key areas that matter and track the status of each deal using a report that shows red, amber, or green for the key area.

Points to consider

A problem I've observed with playbooks is that they can get far too large. Another problem is that the approval process's focus on the big issues can be the first time that the deal team has stepped back and considered the deal as a whole.

One way to address this is to identify for particular deal types what topics really matter to the organisation, and then use this structure for risk reviews, reporting status through the negotiations, and as part of the approval process. You can start with a simple one-page document that is updated alongside the draft contract itself.

Try to keep the issues to fewer than fifteen, ideally fewer than ten. Whitling them down is an excellent way to start to build a broader consensus around what really matters. The issues should represent the different parts of your organisation who are affected by the contract, so not just legal, but also finance, operations and commercial.

Summary

In this chapter, I've covered the basics you need to put in place for your contracting process:

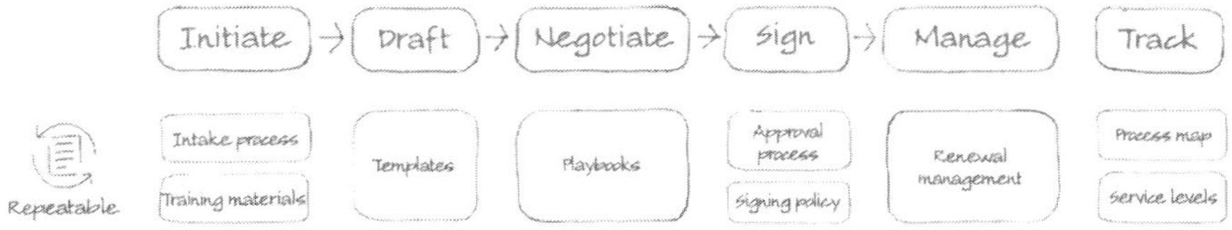

None of the parts will be great at first, and that's OK. Greatness comes from iteratively improving them over time, and there will always be things to improve. Most importantly, once you've completed these steps, you will be ready for automation, which is much more fun. Onwards!

Chapter 5 Robots: Core Principles

Now that you've got the basics in place, let's look at applying technology. At this point, I would gently remind you that there are no silver bullets, and you're not going to solve everything with a shiny new system, no matter how breathlessly the salesperson describes its features. With that in mind, I will start with an overview of the different types of available systems and what they do, discuss contract lifecycle management, breakdown the technology into its underlying components, explain where AI might fit in, and highlight the value of using what you already have. In the next chapter, I will detail which systems to focus on and how to get the most from them.

Using technology to help with contracting dates back to at least the 1970s, but there has been a recent explosion in the options available for automating your contracting process. Depending on your predilections, you'll either consider the range of options to be deeply daunting or like a sweet shop to your inner child.

The truth is that not all that glitters is gold. Putting a system in place doesn't necessarily mean it will have a significant impact, either because it will turn out only to fix a small part of the overall problem (which is common) or it will not get used (which is even more common).

What technology is available?

"***Men have become the tools of their tools.***" - Henry David Thoreau

There isn't a general recognised category of "Contract Tech", but beyond just email and Word, which let's be honest are the tools used most in practice, there is technology for sales, procurement, and legal teams related to contracts.

To try to make sense of the very noisy technology world, here's a map of how the different products fit into the stages of the contracting process:

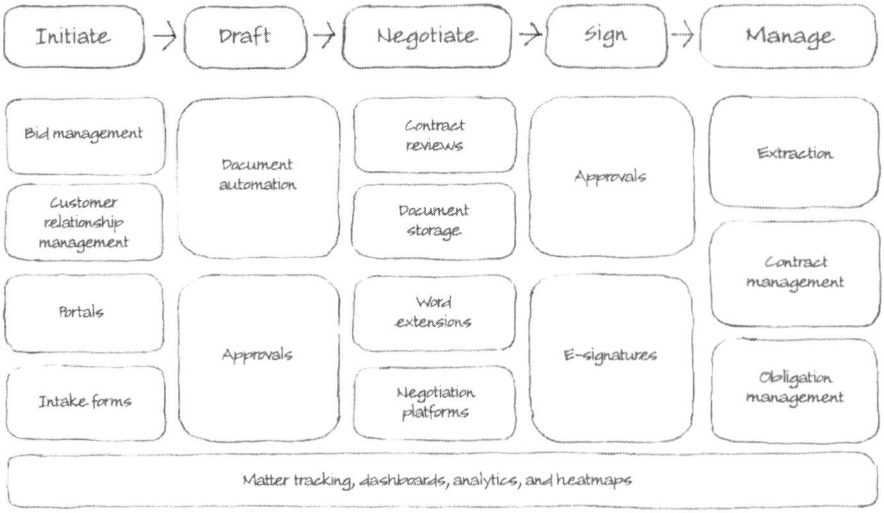

Figure 11 - Types of contract technology

Here's what they do:

Initiate

- **Bid management**: A general term for a range of procurement systems covering requests for proposals, auctions, and other bid processes.

- **Customer relationship management**: A system used by the sales team for tracking leads and opportunities. Opportunities may eventually become contracts, so this can be a feeder system for the contracting process and even the record system for the outcome.

- **Portal**: A single place on your intranet for the business (and contracting) team to go to for self-service resources and help.

- **Intake forms**: Forms for the business to complete to get help from the contracting team, ensuring that the relevant information is gathered and the contracting team can immediately get going, and potentially starting a matter-tracking process.

Draft

- **Document automation**: Systems that let the contracting team (or the business) generate tailored contracts based on answers to questions.

- **Drafting approvals**: Systems to automate the approvals process for drafted contracts (such as those created by the business) or approve the business's instructions.

Negotiate

- **Contract reviews**: AI tools to flag issues in contracts on the other side's paper that are based on whether particular types of clauses appear (or not). Some tools now try to mark-up the contract too.

- **Document storage**: Online places to store draft agreements (and potentially emails) so that other team members can access them.

- **Word extensions**: Additional buttons for Word to help lawyers format, check and update contracts during negotiations, as well as access clause databases.

- **Negotiation platforms**: Online negotiation tools that allow participants to amend contracts in the browser rather than send documents back and forth by email.

Sign

- **Signing approvals**: For collecting approvals before signature on finalised contracts.

- **E-signatures**: Systems for signing documents online, avoiding the need for printing and wet-ink signatures.

Manage

- **Extraction**: AI tools for extracting key data points from signed contracts or reviewing a collection of signed contracts to find provisions.

- **Contract management**: Systems for storing signed contracts and associated data.

- **Obligation management**: Systems for tracking the performance of obligations under contracts.

Track

- **Matter tracking and dashboards**: Systems for tracking the status of all your deals, usually with a dashboard showing performance against key measures.

- **Heatmaps**: Data analytics tools to display which parts of your contracts are negotiated most.

Contract Lifecycle Management

"***NEW SYSTEM MEANS NEW PROBLEMS***" - John Gall[72]

Not all the tools described above are necessarily distinct. You can buy a system that gives you many different capabilities, generally referred to as contract lifecycle management (CLM). Whether you should do this is a trade-off between two competing approaches by the suppliers, who offer either:

- **Point solutions**: systems that just do one thing and not much else and are often very good at what they do.

- **End-to-end solutions**: CLM systems that support the contracting process from initiation through to contract management[73]. They may not be as good at any particular activity as a point solution, but they have the advantage of connecting all the parts.

In the first edition of this book I was relatively neutral on which of the two approaches to take. After a number of poor experiences with clients' CLM systems slowing Radiant Law down in both supporting and improving their contracting processes, I have stronger opinions.

Let's start with some advantages of choosing a CLM:

- **Ticks boxes**: CLMs offer lots of features, so they give you many of the tools that I will be discussing in the next chapter through one project.

---

[72] From the excellent book Systemantics, which should be handed to anyone telling you that their system will solve all your problems. I wrote a longer piece on CLMs and Systemantics here: https://www.radiantlaw.com/resources/the-system-strikes-back

[73] Often, these suppliers came out of the contract management world and expanded to include earlier stages of the contracting process to cover the full contract lifecycle.

- **Integrated data**: CLMs make it easier to integrate data between the steps in the contracting process and track the end-to-end performance, while avoiding the need to "double-key" data.

- **Pick and choose**: You don't have to use every feature of a CLM, in fact we have often seen companies only use a handful of the available parts. This mitigates some of the concerns that I will cover, but if you are only using a few features, you may not get the advantage of integrated data.

- **Fewer tools**: We all have too many tools in our lives. Having one place to go for contracting may mean fewer tools to train on and encourage using. CLMs are more likely to offer a unified design and user experience. This will have more impact for those spending most of their time working on contracting; where it's just one part of the user's job then it probably won't make much difference.

Unfortunately, there are also issues:

- **Underpowered features**: The point of CLMs is to cover the entire contracting process and the development of CLMs has been heavily influenced by procurement processes. Companies have sought all-singing, all-dancing systems, and suppliers have responded by adding every conceivable feature. Unfortunately, this means that each feature tends to be underpowered compared to point solutions. For some features, this doesn't matter. For some like document automation and workflow, this can materially undermine the value of the system.

- **Large IT Projects tend to fail**: IT implementation projects have a terrible success rate, and this gets worse the more ambitious they are. Going in, organisations tend to overestimate the end value and their understanding of needs and current practices; they tend to underestimate the total costs. Over the course of the project, time tends to slip and costs increase, and it's easy to get trapped in a spiral of upping the promises for future benefits while struggling to deliver basic features. Meanwhile, reality turns out to be far messier than hoped and the number of edge cases explode. Successful large systems tend to be built by expanding working small systems, but CLM projects often try to skip that key step.

- **Future inflexibility**: Even if you successfully implement your shiny new system, there will be challenges coming down the line. The more complex the system, the more brittle it will be and commensurately harder to make changes. Consultants are expensive, internal developers are in demand, and even if you are using a no-code/low-code platform, the knowledge of how it works will sit with a few people, who probably have other things to do (and may have left the organisation). The result is that we have found CLMs to be blockers to continuous improvement. A related issue is that CLMs tend to represent the opinions of their developers about what matters. You may get a nice dashboard out of the box, but the value of the metrics will tend to diminish over time as you move past the immediate issues that are revealed by the data and need to dig deeper into what is going on.

- **Contracts aren't the point**: CLMs are orientated around contracts, but there is far more to the relationship with your customers and suppliers than what is represented in the contract. At Radiant Law we track hundreds of datapoints about our clients needs and the performance of our services, and the vast majority of these do not appear anywhere in our contracts with clients. There are good reasons for HR contracts to be addressed in HR systems, sales contracts to be subsumed in CRMs and so on. Legal teams cover more than contracts in the work they do, so should the CLM also cover other areas such as litigation? This takes us to another issue—which department is going to own the system? Joint decision making is hard, but if you don't involve all the other departments affected by the system then it is unlikely to meet their needs and you may find it tends to be ignored or even undermined in practice.

This is not to say that CLMs are never the right answer. For larger organisation, the sheer volumes involved may mean that heavyweight systems are hard to avoid. And if you have hit the limits of integrating point solutions then a CLM may solve real issues.

My advice, though, is to err on the side of lightweight solutions in the first instance (and, as ever, don't get stuck trying to make a choice). We prefer point solutions at Radiant Law because we regularly change our minds on the best approach, as we continue to experiment. We also work in unusual ways (which is why we are the fastest supplier on the planet at turning contracts), so we find the opinions implicit in large systems to be unhelpful. It has meant, though, that we had to develop expertise in integrating systems to allow them to work together.

If you are still keen to go down the CLM path, a couple of points to bear in mind:

- **Future changes**: Try to chose as flexible systems as possible, for modelling both the contracting process and the data.

You will keep discovering new pathways for your processes and data points that you will want to track[74].

- **Make your contracts actionable**: Both parties will have obligations under your contracts, and these need to be complied with as part of the relationship. Making these points actionable and actually actioned is a real challenge. CLMs should be helping here, not just storing documents after the deal is done. Consider how these points are going to be extracted, shared, and tracked. [75]

[74] For workflow, you ideally want a system that can model the full business process model and notation (BPMN) standard. For data, you want to be able to define the data that is captured (including the data model). More generally, no-code/low-code is generally preferable to requiring programming (right up to the point when it can't do what you need), and keep an eye on how easy it is to update automated templates. On the data point, the brilliant Andy Wishart has a nice model for the different types of data that you should consider: the content of the contract, the performance of the contracting process, the performance of the parties after signature, and data to support decisions such as playbooks and risks.

[75] Thanks to Jeff Carr for emphasising this point.

Case Study: The Upgrade

A company sold complex products, not helped by the sales team regularly going off-piste and creating new variations. The finance team struggled to track the deals, and millions of pounds were lost each year due to poor invoicing. The company introduced a new intake system that was integrated with the contract management system and used a complex form that had to be completed by the sales team.

The company collected better data, but there were issues: the system's champion left the company and wasn't replaced. The integration between the systems turned out to be brittle, meaning that updates to the intake form often required changes by multiple teams of programmers (who had other priorities). The form collected more data than necessary, making it unpopular with the sales team. The project was also underfunded.

Eighteen months later, the contracting process was still slower than before the system had been introduced.

Case Study 5 - The Upgrade

Databases, workflows, document transformation and beyond

"Automation is not about replacing people. It's about replacing tasks." - Stewart Butterfield

It's easy to be overwhelmed by all the technology available, but the systems are generally pretty straightforward and usually combine one or more of five core technologies:

- **Databases**: a structured way of saving data,
- **Workflow**: a way to manage the flow of tasks between different people (and automate parts of the journey),

- **Document transformation**: a way of creating documents and converting them to different formats,

- **Finding and extracting**: simple search, now being enhanced by machine learning and even generative AI, and

- **GenAI as fairy dust**: generative AI is starting to be sprinkled across everything. In some places it might even help.

Not exactly rocket science.

This breakdown gives us some more insight into the point solution v CLM debate. In an ideal world, you wouldn't want to keep your data in more than one database, and you would like to store as much data as possible. Right now, we're usually throwing away most of the data associated with contracting (or at least it's inaccessible), and we're generally not using the data that is to hand. Even in the most sophisticated of end-to-end CLM systems, the level of data analytics is pretty crude. All the same, keeping structured data in one place and ensuring that contract documents are easily accessible will have an advantage in the long term.

Similarly, with workflow, there is value in modelling and controlling the flow of the end-to-end contracting process. Taken to its logical conclusion, this means bringing all the participants in the negotiation together on a negotiation platform, thus removing the need for email and Word. It's a great idea, but it has a serious problem. In every negotiation, the other party will have to adopt the system instead of continuing with their usual way of working. Anyone who has tried to roll out a system with their team will understand how challenging this is. Some suppliers are working on making their negotiation platform as simple as possible, and perhaps one day this will get real traction, but not yet.

Even if you scale back your ambitions and just try to model your internal processes, there can be real challenges. Expect the refinement to take far longer than you bargained for, as reality turns out to be highly complicated and the path of emails convoluted. Be careful, therefore, about how much you bite off at first, and bear in mind that a bit of flexibility, such as using email for some parts of the process, may be better than trying to move everything into one system.

The document transformation elements (e.g., document automation and e-signatures) underline how document-centric the contracting process is, despite automation. Even if companies can find their signed contracts, they are often scanned PDFs that require optical character recognition[76] and AI to extract data points at scale.

This brings us to the thorny topic of AI.

Artificial intelligence

"AI might be a powerful technology, but things won't get better simply by adding AI." - Vivienne Ming

If ever there were an example of a silver bullet wannabe, it's AI. The potential of expert systems, then machine learning and natural language processing, and now generative AI, has been greeted with much excitement by customers who hope it will fix all their problems; and plenty of legal tech suppliers are keen to sell them anything. The only problem with this union of demand and supply are the limits to the underlying technology, leading to a lot of talk, but not so much action. Will this change with generative AI?

---

[76] Optical character recognition or OCR is an often-wrong way of turning a scan into searchable text.

In Chapter 3, I proposed a model for knowledge work with the spectrum between routine work and innovative work. Before exploring AI, and with an eye on trying to make contracting knowledge work more routine, let's consider what we are trying to achieve:

- **Create great relationships**: The purpose of contracting is to create great commercial relationships. Relationships are ultimately between people, and even commercial relationships between companies are created and implemented by people. We want to have more fruitful and thoughtful discussions as part of contracting, giving personal relationships a chance to grow. We therefore want the contracting process to put people at the forefront, not hide them behind technology. That said, if there are tools that can help us improve how we create relationships, for example by improving the tone of communications or the way we approach thorny issues, then that might be valuable.

- **Deliver reliability and consistency**: As discussed in Chapter 3, there is a huge value in reliably dealing with key points in your contracts and being consistent across your portfolio. Any technology and other tools you use should help improve reliability and consistency.

- **Get rid of busy work**: As noted in the "Automated" part of RADICAL contracting, there is no glory in doing mechanical tasks by hand, which could be better performed by automation. So if we can automate these tasks, while neither undermining the creation of relationships nor reliability and consistency, we should welcome the help.

- **Handle novel work**: Although we are trying to make work more routine and reduce the need for unnecessary innovative work, we will still regularly face novel situations. Tools that can help explore new contracting scenarios and think them through could be of great benefit. Tools that help with new activities like analysing data (which I didn't learn how to do at law school) could also be game changers.

- **Make knowledge explicit**: Creating knowledge assets and making tacit knowledge explicit is hard. If these tools could help us simplify contracts, or explore topics by prompting our brains, that might make all the difference in getting going with improvements.

What is AI?

AI has a long cyclical history of bold promises for a new approach, a failure to live up to the promise, a subsequent winter of low investment, and then the next cycle starts. That doesn't mean there hasn't been progress, but it does mean that a certain scepticism is healthy, especially now at the time of writing when we are at the height of generative AI enthusiasm. Sometimes it really is different, but the onus is on the enthusiasts to make their case.

There are three AI approaches relevant to contracting: expert systems, machine learning, and generative AI.

Expert systems were an early approach that tried to distil tacit knowledge into a set of rules for how to handle scenarios, walking the user through a set of questions to determine the answer. This approach turned out to be too fragile to handle the complexity of many problems, but document automation (which I will discuss in the next chapter) can be viewed as a simple expert system that produces a tailored contract based on the answers to questions. It is a tool to capture "if-then" thinking and works brilliantly when the range of possible outcomes are well understood. Document automation, in other words, is a reliable deterministic system to produce consistent outcomes for work that has been made routine.

Machine learning was a very different approach. Rather than the programmer trying to figure out every rule in advance, the system was trained on large volumes of example data to identify the rules to apply. This turned out to be most useful in contracting for classifying clauses. In practice, there are a staggering number of ways that lawyers have come up with to say the same thing. Searching for key words breaks down in practice, although you can still find a governing law clause reliably enough, so hard coded search rules failed (echoes of the expert system problem). However, if you train a system with enough examples of a particular clause type, you can create a model that fairly reliably finds that type of clause in a contract. If you train a model for all of the types of clauses you are interested in identifying, you now have a way of extracting those clauses from a contract.

There are two places in the map where machine learning helps:

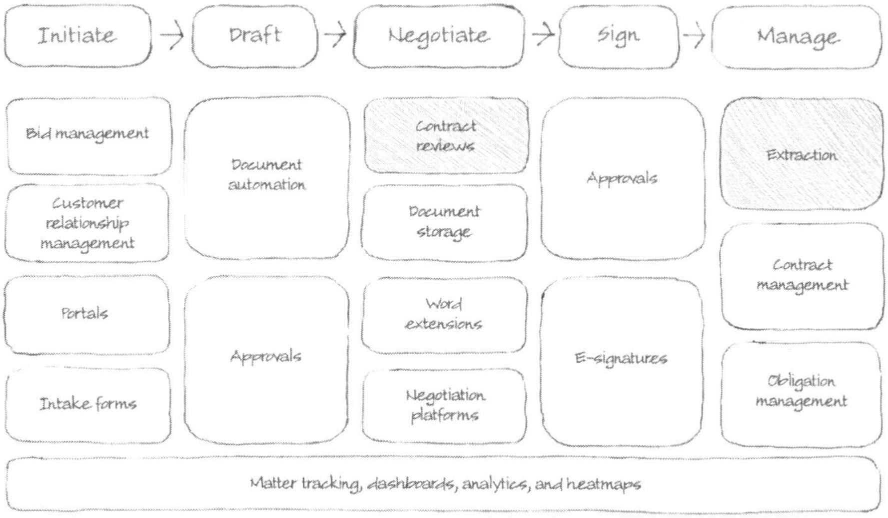

Figure 12 - Where machine learning fits in

Contract review: These are tools to review the other side's paper to spot issues. These tools are clever. They let you build rules for whether you want to see, or not see, clauses of a particular type and then warn you about what they find (so combining machine learning with expert system-like rules). The results are a bit crude, both because the systems aren't 100% reliable at finding clauses of a particular type and because with machine learning the system doesn't know what the clause means. With just machine learning, you still need to read and mark up the agreement and then negotiate it to fix any problems found.

These tools can speed up the review process and provide another pair of eyes, which improves consistency if you get a lot of contracts of a particular type. But this raises another question: why are you receiving so many agreements on the other side's paper? The best solution would be to use your paper instead[77].

Extraction: This covers tools with two use cases. The first is extracting data as part of getting contracts into a contract management system. The second is for document reviews as part of major one-off events (legislative changes, acquisitions, etc.). These tools help, but before we consider it revolutionary, let's be clear about what's going on: you are replacing paralegals with a faster and cheaper tool. What you do with the data is more important than how you review the contracts.

What changed with generative AI?

---

[77] There is another problem associated with the system ideally needing to be configured for your organisation's particular concerns and risk appetite (rather than relying on the system defaults), which is that the configuration is only justified when using it multiple times for the same type of agreement. Again, better to use your own terms.

Generative AI

Generative AI (GenAI) is a new approach that also uses training data, but far more than was required by machine learning[78]. It's a mind-blowing experience to play with GenAI. If you haven't already tried it, I recommend you do. It can draft contracts, extract clauses, and suggest points to negotiate. Its output always looks impressive. Tone and grammar can be excellent, text looks convincing, and it is always confident. Sometimes the output is correct too.

There are points that you should be aware of with GenAI:

- **GenAI is inconsistent**: GenAI uses a prediction model that generates answers that look right. That can include contracts. It's not a miracle; it's digested an awful lot of awful contracts in training, and is spewing out text that looks like the contracts it trained on. Moving past the problem with being trained on the dire drafting that is prevalent in our industry, the answer just has to look like what a human would produce. Unfortunately, the output, however carefully you hone the prompt and reduce the temperature[79], will be different every time, often internally inconsistent, and if you are drafting or analysing a contract

---

[78] "Generative AI, including Large Language Models (LLMs), is a cutting-edge technology that creates new content—text, images, music, and more—by learning patterns from existing data. For lawyers, LLMs can draft documents, summarize case law, generate legal research, and automate routine tasks, significantly enhancing productivity and accuracy." Explanation courtesy of ChatGPT, which may be biased.

[79] Temperature is a setting to increase or decrease how random the output is. More random outputs may be more interesting and creative, but with the consistency needed in contracting, variability is a bug not a feature.

it will randomly introduce issues likely to lead to lengthy and unhelpful negotiations.

- **GenAI doesn't really reason:** This is a hotly debated point, because GenAI can appear to reason, but what it's really doing is serving up reasoning embedded in the text it trained on[80]. If you show it novel problems, it will tend to fall over. That said, GenAI can do some level of clause and contract level interpretation and will sometimes get it right. This is a significant advance on machine learning.

- **GenAI needs to be checked:** Given that we are trying to achieve consistency and reliability, it looks like the output of GenAI for the foreseeable future will always need to be checked. This is very different to determinative systems such as document automation, where if you get it right creating the template, you do not need to check every output.

- **GenAI can be hard to check**: Getting past the problem with facts (GenAI makes them up all the time), GenAI models have been trained to give plausible answers, and they are very convincing.[81] The grammar is excellent, the tone feels

---

[80] GenAI is also a black-box system, meaning that you can't get visibility of why it gave a particular response. You can force it to show its reasoning when answering a question, but the reasoning needs to be checked as well as the answer, and the reasoning is also meant to look good rather than be right—it may not stand up to scrutiny or actually support the answer.

[81] Because GenAI is producing answers that look right, with little regard for whether they are right, a GenAI system on its own can never be trusted. You will have heard enough about, or experienced, the "hallucinations" problem to hopefully know that it is utterly unreliable. That doesn't mean that a system incorporating GenAI cannot reliably produce correct factual answer. Smart people are figuring out how to connect GenAI to trusted sources of data and force it to use that data. They are also building systems that can show links to the

right, and each sentence generally parses. Meanwhile, humans tend to switch off when reading something that looks right, especially when it is a wall of text.[82] Contracts are highly technical documents, where the parts need to work with each other and things that are missing can be just as important as things that are included. We tend, in contracting practice, to assume that what we are reviewing is at least rigorous, even if it includes positions that we may not agree with. We also tend to be bad at spotting when things are missing. The upshot is that relying on humans to check contracts drafted whole by GenAI is particularly risky, and underlines why well-honed templates are so important.

Given those points, here are some principles that I suggest applying:

- **Use deterministic systems where possible:** Given the need for reliability and consistency, it is always preferable to use a system that will give you the same result each time, all things being equal. Most organisations haven't yet done what is possible with deterministic systems such as document automation. If you can make these work, they are preferable. However, these systems don't cover everything involved in the practice of contracting. Not all situations are predictable in advance or come up regularly enough to justify the investment. Some things can't be collapsed into if-then statements, and deterministic systems can be hard to

data sources so you can check them. Perhaps this might also be possible when analysing your contracts, but this is not a solved problem at the time of writing.

[82] There is an associated issue of plausible answers triggering a problematic part of human reasoning. We tend to think by analogy. When we see a system doing something that we have only experienced humans doing, we may assume that it can therefore do other things that humans can do. This is dangerous, because GenAI can and will fail at other tasks that "should" be trivial to a human.

set up and maintain. So, I'm not arguing that there is no space for GenAI, just that if a deterministic system will solve the problem, err towards using that approach rather than GenAI.

- **Harness iterative improvements:** Back when I was a "real" lawyer doing deals, I observed that a novel clause I wrote usually needed to be improved over about three deals before I was happy for it to become a standard. It's not that it didn't work the first time, I just tended to find room for improvement over the next two, before the law of diminishing returns kicked in. I've observed this pattern elsewhere in my work, and it has led me to value having a limited number of generic assets that keep being improved, rather than a large repository of examples. Not only do I get the benefit of improving the asset, rather than continually creating new things, but it also becomes easier to share with others (including because it doesn't require contextual knowledge of the situation where it was first used).

- **Data structures matter:** Given the value in improving things, rather than creating everything afresh, it matters where you keep things, including nuggets of knowledge. If you can't find something fast when you need it, then it has no value. If it doesn't live in a place where its relationship to other assets and nuggets is also represented, then it is harder to use. GenAI is going to perform better where it has access to structured knowledge; your team will benefit immediately. I discussed the importance of knowledge management in Chapter 3, GenAI makes it more important, not less.

- **Prompt your brain not the machine**: I've found it most useful to treat GenAI as a tool to prompt my brain. If I ask it to give me a list of points, it seems to trigger my thinking and I can quickly add, remove and clean the list up. It's not only far faster than starting with a blank piece of paper, it's so much easier (thinking IS hard) and leads to a much better result. What I've found, therefore, is that with the right data structure (where I can save the output), GPT is a fabulous tool to stimulate my brain and help solve the gnarly problem of making tacit knowledge explicit. Humans may be bad at dealing with walls of text, but asking for bullets as a starting point for thinking works brilliantly for me.

So where might GenAI usefully fit in?

Drafting

Unless and until the significant issues with GenAI can be resolved, I strongly recommend that you don't use GenAI to create new agreements each time. You will be much better off using templates and document automation. However, there are places where we have found GenAI to be helpful:

- drafting novel clauses,
- creating first drafts of service descriptions where there is too much variability to use document automation—we have combined document automation for the framework with GenAI to provide starting text for the different sections,
- creating new templates and refining existing templates as part of making them short, clear, reasonable, and relevant, and

- automating templates—I've written a lot of code with GenAI, and have had some success in accelerating the template automation process for document automation.

Negotiating

Our goal is to reduce negotiations so that the focus is on the key commercial issues. Although we are starting to see examples of GenAI based system being used to mark up agreements or deal with track changes, the quality so far has been abysmal. Even if the quality issues are resolved, without real reasoning and given the propensity to output different answers each time, I fear that GenAI will lead to more negotiations of the wrong points. Some envisage computers negotiating against each other, but I don't see how that would help create great relationships; our goal is not to automate current dysfunctional practices. Areas where I think GenAI could help are:

- exploring negotiation options for difficult issues in advance,
- improving the tone of communications, and
- for novel contracting situations, identifying possible issues with drafts, provided that judgement is still applied to which points to raise—I expect that the machine learning systems that I described above will be enhanced with GenAI.

Interpretation

I expect that GenAI will significantly enhance our ability to review large volumes of signed contracts for particular provisions and help interpret larger contracts. Obviously, you need to find these contracts first, so start with a contract management system to hold your signed contracts. Given the issues with reasoning and reliability, you will want to still check the answers, but I expect contract review projects to get easier. Whether this will have a major impact is unclear. We should still be aiming for easily understood contracts and consistency across our contract portfolio, so templates matter just as much. We also want our contracts to be actionable and actually actioned. Identifying points in a contract is only useful when we do something with the outcomes—this is ultimately a process, rather than technology, problem.

Analysis and improvements

This book is full of topics that are not normally taught in law school (although this is improving with the more progressive educational institutions). GenAI can be a helpful assistant in carrying out data analysis, thinking through options for improvements, and learning about new areas. I encourage you to experiment with how it might help you.

I've given a number of potential use cases above, but they are fundamentally enhancing how we do tasks, not replacing the job. So is GenAI really a gamechanger?

GenAI is likely to be embedded across our IT tools, and at times may help. Given the importance of creating human relationships and the current limits of the technology, we should be focusing on how GenAI can assist us to think more deeply and do the right things, not how to replace people with automation to mindlessly continue doing the wrong things. We should, in other words, be aiming for bionic lawyers, not robot lawyers, and think of GenAI as a tool not a solution. In this light, if used well then it appears GenAI can help, but the breathless claims of some that junior lawyers are done for, or that everything is different, seem unlikely to me.

Forms

"All this red tape and form-filling. That's what comes of a bureaucratic state. Can't go where you like and do as you please anymore! Somebody's always asking questions." - Agatha Christie

Let's switch gears, and talk about forms. Structured forms will still play a key role in collecting the data you need to support contracts, including intake forms and document automation. Forms allow you to get exactly the information you need, validate answers, and take control of how you receive instructions. Unfortunately, as I noted in Chapter 4, your business users don't tend to wake up in the morning eager to start filling forms and probably preferred the old hand waving they previously used to start the process. It is incumbent on you to make the experience as simple and painless as possible, even if it will never be a pleasure. The following is quite detailed, so feel free to come back to this section when you need to create a form.

Creating forms

You should agonise over your questions:

- **Everything you need**: the form needs to be complete, in that you should not need to ask any follow-up questions to complete the first stage of the work, at least for the common deal-types. This means that you first need to understand your deal-types.

- **Minimal number of questions**: despite that, you should only ask the questions that are relevant to the work that needs to be done. Use conditional questions, as in questions that only appear depending on answers to previous questions. Avoid unnecessary questions where the answer is already known (e.g., the company number of a group company).

- **Short, clear questions**: the questions should be as short as possible. Every word you add slows down the user and adds "cognitive burden". Try not to use more than seven words, and use terminology that the user is familiar with.

- **Explanatory notes**: add notes only where needed, but again keep them as short as possible. Your goal is to never need to give training. Explain where a user can find information if it's not obvious.

- **Logical ordering**: the questions should appear in a logical order, but try putting the easiest questions at the top.

- **General question at the end**: you should have an open question at the end to allow the user to provide relevant information that you hadn't envisaged when you created the form.

- **Every question should be mandatory**: in order to know that you have all the answers, every question should be made mandatory. The general question at the end should be a mandatory "Is there anything else we should know?" with a yes/no answer that reveals the text box.

You should also agonise over the field types and other form elements that you use:

- **Text fields v text boxes**: use a text field for a single line of text. Use a text box (text area) if the text is likely to be more than a few words.

- **Checkboxes v radio buttons**: check boxes are for when you can select more than one option. Radio buttons are for when you can only choose one option. Do not use a single checkbox on its own as you won't be able to tell if it was overlooked. Do not have a default option on a radio button as you, again, won't be able to tell if it was overlooked.

- **Dropdowns**: dropdowns save space but make it harder for the user to see all options. Only use dropdowns if you have more than four options. Multi-select dropdowns are also fiddly to complete, so try to use checkboxes where you can.

- **Data validation**: use date fields for dates, number fields for numbers etc to help ensure that the data is entered accurately. Where it needs to be entered in a very specific format, use specific rules for data validation.

- **Avoid placeholder text**: don't use placeholder text in the form unless it's the only way to show notes with your software. It tends to confuse users.

- **Progress bars**: the user should know where they are in the form. If you split the form into multiple pages, include a progress bar.

- **Action buttons**: action buttons should appear at the bottom of the form. The label on the action button should be meaningful and not "Submit" —what is going to happen for the user when they click it?

Choosing your form software

Given the points above, you need to be careful that the systems you are considering have all the features you need. This is the first of the major gotchas, because many systems out there are missing some of these:

- **Input types:** the software should be able to handle the following: text field, text box (text area), radio buttons, checkboxes, dropdowns (both single-select and multiselect if you have long lists), dates, numbers (both integers and decimals), and attachments (with multiple files).

- **Conditional questions**: you need to be able to turn on/off questions depending on previous answers.

- **Mandatory questions:** you want to be able to require the user to answer each question before submitting. Conditional questions need to be capable of being made mandatory, only when they appear.

- **Notes:** it will help to be able to add explanations, although clear questions are preferable.

Other points to consider:

- **How the form looks:** forms are bad enough without being ugly too. Is the software beautiful? If not out of the box, how much control do you have over how it looks? This is a double-edged sword, as good design skills are rare and corporate PowerPoints attest to how dangerous it is to give users the ability to change look and feel, but are you doomed to a hideous experience?

- **Proliferating tickets**: even the best forms don't get answered perfectly every time, so consider how you address the back and forth with your business users including asking for more information. Will this happen within the system? Watch out for multiple instructions if you are asking the user to update data (and does the system even allow for updates?), and consider how you are going to handle the inevitable duplicates.

- **Structured data**: you will probably want to analyse the data to see what is happening so consider how easy this is to do in your system and how you can export the data when you have new questions.

User testing and improvements

The following is true for all technology projects, but it will be a particular issue for forms, where you are likely to have the most control over what users see.

The starting point is that you have no idea what your users will find confusing. However much time you spend perfecting your form, as soon as it is in the wild you will have stumped users. The only solution is to do extensive user testing, and not just with your lawyers. Get typical users to fill in the form and just watch them (using shared screens if necessary). See where they get stuck and ask them to talk through what they are doing as they do it.

You will uncover issue after issue, so assume that you are going to run an iterative process until a new user (so you need multiple test subjects) can fly through it (and see below for ongoing changes).

Once your form is being used, you are still not done. First, however much you test the form, issues will come up. Second, there is always room for improvement. Third, your organisation will continue to change. As part of the Refinement stage, you will be running a continuous improvement process, but it is worth considering now how changes to your forms will be supported.

If you've hired someone to set it up, will they be available to make changes in the future? Have you budgeted for ongoing support? Will you be able to get changes made in days not weeks (or even months, if at all)? If it's being done internally, will the person who set it up always be available to make changes? Can someone else help?

How do you find opportunities for improvement? This comes down to how you respond to failure. When the form isn't completed correctly, do you blame the user, fall back on mandatory training courses, or dig deeper into what is going on and figure out how the form can be improved? Points which might trigger your inner detective:

- incomplete answers, including users getting around mandatory fields by inserting spaces,
- incorrect answers or the wrong documents being attached, or
- instructions changing after the lawyer digs in to do the work.

Perhaps also talk to the users who are getting it right? How could it be made even easier for them? Stay curious!

Further considerations

"Simplicity is the ultimate sophistication." - Leonardo da Vinci

Some other points to consider as you adopt new technology:

- **Fewer tools:** Although users have lots of tools available, they only use a handful in practice. The usage tails off fast after the first two or three they use daily. If a user isn't using an application daily, they will tend to forget about it. If you think about what lawyers use, the first two positions are inevitably taken by email and Word. If you are hoping your users will adopt a new system, think about what else it will be competing with and whether other tools need to be dropped rather than just accumulating more.

- **Flexibility v completeness:** It's tempting with a new system to seek completeness—making sure that it does everything. Be aware, though, that your use cases will change, and in practice, what you think are vital priorities may go unused (we're regularly wrong on this front). We've found that giving users flexible and general tools is usually more helpful in the long run than a specific system[83].

- **Start with what you have:** Your IT department probably doesn't care as much about your problems as you might wish. They have a lot on their hands, and the contracting process generally isn't their top priority. Instead, they're trying to use fewer systems, introduce better integrations, improve security, and get business users actually using the systems they begged for. So before reaching for a shiny new system, consider using what already exists in your environment. You probably have a central place to store things (SharePoint or Google Sites), a ticketing system for intake, data analytics tools, etc. Using what you have is your best starting option, unless you're ready to sign up to a cloud service with a credit card, can take advantage of another department's project, or can create an overwhelming business case for your project.

- **Get going with something:** We regularly see companies caught up in complex evaluations of the many systems available in the market. The larger the company is, the worse this process can be. Implementing pretty much

[83] It's no accident that Microsoft has done as well as it has with the Office suite, and Office 365 offers powerful automation systems.

anything is better than analysis paralysis. Don't let your ambitions get ahead of practicalities. A late and expensive project that cannot deliver on what it promised is a poor way to win hearts and minds. Better to crack on with something simple and build on it over time.

- **Open source:** Open source is one of the most potent technology developments of our time, yet it has a poor reputation in some quarters. There has been a Cambrian explosion of software libraries and systems, often better than the commercial alternatives. Legal tech has been mainly proprietary to date, and any open systems or standards have been the exception rather than the rule. However, we're now starting to see significant systems emerge that are not only extremely powerful but also free. If you're having problems getting IT's attention, try asking them to install an open-source system for you. The most important of these for our purposes at the time of writing is Docassemble, a document automation system[84].

- **A word about Word:** Finally, we should talk about Word. It's the primary tool for contracts and used by almost every lawyer[85], but it's also the most abused technology. I shudder

---

[84] We may have gone backwards on this front since the first edition. Although there are powerful LLM models appearing (thanks in no small part to Meta releasing the Llama models), at the time of writing the second edition, the conversation has moved to closed GenAI models, which can be expensive especially given how many software tool seem to be selling AI as an additionally-chargeable feature. Let's see how this plays out; I remain bullish for the value of open source systems.

[85] There are also those using Google Docs, and some are even negotiating contracts directly on these documents. This requires the parties to be comfortable showing their changes as they are made, but if you can make it work, it's a great

to think how much time has been wasted by lawyers fiddling around with formatting documents. To give you a sense of the time lost, we've built extensions for Word, adding features that save lawyers from having to make manual changes, and it now takes us about half the time to mark up a contract as it did previously. Your team can also save vast amounts of time by just learning to use Word properly and there are many excellent training courses on the internet. If your team isn't using standard styles templates across documents, keyboard shortcuts, automated cross-referencing, and track changes, they're doing it wrong.

Summary

This chapter introduced a wide variety of specialist systems, questioned the enthusiasm for CLMs, and broke down the underlying technology. I think I was quite measured about AI, but I expect many will disagree with my conclusions. I explained how to approach the horrors of forms. Most importantly, I recommended starting with what you have already and keeping it simple.

As exciting as technology projects can be, there is a considerable risk of overblown expectations failing to be met by the technology. Implementation is also part of the challenge— you need long-term cultural change to ensure you get value. Starting small and evolving lets you avoid costly mistakes and get going faster. With that in mind, let's explore which systems help.

---

potential improvement on emailing drafts back and forth. And there are still pockets of Word Perfect users out there. I'm not sure I can help you if you are one of them.

Chapter 6 Robots: The Steps

You don't need to implement every type of technology, and probably never will. The ones that we recommend at the Robots stage are:

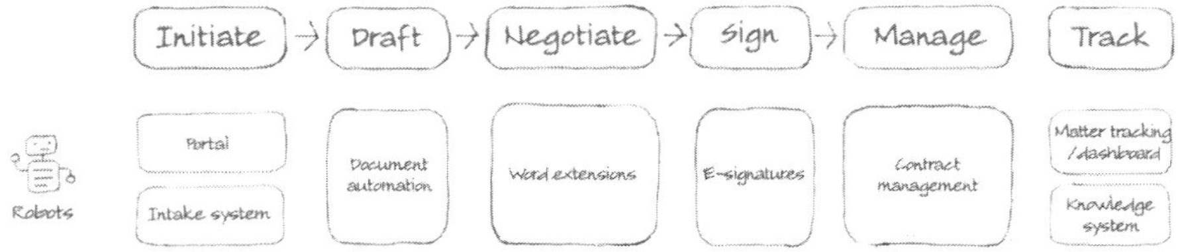

Figure 13 - Robot stage steps

Some of these are specialist contracting tools, but many of them can be covered by repurposing existing platforms within your organisation, at least in the first instance. You will also probably still be using email and Word for the foreseeable future.

I selected these systems because they are the ones that have a real impact. A simple version of each will be good enough for now. It's generally not that hard to migrate to a better system in the future (compared to the effort required in the initial automation), so try to just get going.

Portals and wikis

Problem

How do you get the business team to do more themselves?

Solution

Create a portal as a single launch spot for all assistance related to contracting and keep developing it. Use a wiki[86] as a base knowledge repository (your system will probably come with one).

Points to consider

We are all busy, really busy, and if an activity isn't part of our core job description, it will probably not get much attention. Expecting the broader business team to spend much time on the things you care about is going to be an uphill battle. You're therefore going to need to make it as easy as possible for your business users to find what they need when they need it, and it must be highly usable. Expecting enthusiastic participation in complex training or a lot of information to be retained is a bridge too far. Therefore, make sure that they only need to remember one thing: where to go on the intranet when they need contracting help.

Your company inevitably has an intranet, so you don't need to buy a system. Simply adopt what your company is already using, adding a single unified location for contracting needs. You can link to other systems from there, so you don't need full integration to get the benefits of having a single landing spot. You can build the portal out over time and introduce self-help tools, your intake forms for asking for help, and other training and explanatory materials.

While you're doing this, use the same space for sharing materials within your team. I'm a firm believer in using wikis for this as it allows the team to keep evolving the structure of the information, curate valuable resources, and increase everyone's opportunities to contribute to your knowledge management efforts. Although you may wish to keep the information within the contracting team, err on the side of openness.

---

[86] A wiki is a collaborative website that allows users to create, edit, and organize content collectively. The most famous example is Wikipedia, but you can have private wikis and this is now just a feature in software you probably already have in your organisation.

In developing your knowledge management system, think about how it will fit into your organisation:

- **Capabilities**: You will want a system for hosting documents that is linked to pages on the wiki (so you can curate your resources). Microsoft SharePoint or Google Sites and Drive can give you all the capabilities you need.

- **The end-to-end contracting process**: Given that the contracting process spans multiple departments, consider how best to work with the other teams to provide relevant information on the end-to-end process.

- **User testing**: As discussed in Chapter 5 in the context of forms, however simple, easy, and brilliant your materials are, your users will still misunderstand them. There is no faster way to gain humility than to spend a few minutes watching a business user trying to navigate your creation. I recommend regular user testing.

Your system will need ongoing development. Plenty of legal teams have a page on the intranet, but few have a comprehensive, reader-friendly, and current resource. Make someone responsible for keeping it up to date and helpful.

I should mention that there has been some excitement about chatbots as a way for end-users to get answers to questions, and this is only louder with the arrival of GenAI. Chatbots used to be too limited to be that helpful, now they are arguably not limited enough, especially given GenAI's propensity to make things up. There are solutions emerging that limit answers to preapproved FAQs and other documents, and if your team is being sunk by questions then these types of systems might be worth considering.

That said, thoughtful curation of the available information, along with simpler and punchier wording would be a good starting point.

Intake, matter tracking, and dashboards

Problem

How do you keep track of all the deals you are doing?

Solution

Start to automate your tracking of deals, beginning with the intake process itself and then ongoing deal handling. You can then use the data to understand where the deals are coming from, what they relate to, and how best to deploy your team to support contracts.

Points to consider

Having set up the base intake process in the Repeatable stage, now is the time to add automation.

The intake process can start with something as simple as a single email address (e.g., contractintake@company.com). You can set up mailing lists so that multiple team members can see emails, but until you have an automated workflow, make sure there is one person responsible for initial intake and triage to avoid chaos.

Most organisations now have form software in their environments, so going straight to an online form may be a better solution. I discussed how to create forms in Chapter 5. The completed form can be sent to a common email address or your internal messaging system (often Teams, possibly Slack) and ideally will trigger your matter-tracking system once you've implemented it.

Matter-tracking systems allow you to track the status of your deals and capture performance data, too. The status and key metrics can be shown on a dashboard, giving you an overview of workloads and performance. The benefits of these systems include:

- understanding volumes, where requests are coming from, and overall performance of the contracting process,
- helping balance the load across the team,
- understanding where bottlenecks are occurring, and
- potentially coordinating activities across the broader business.

At its simplest, a matter-tracking system can be a shared spreadsheet (or, even better, a Kanban board[87]) showing who is working on what. You can build something simple in a shared spreadsheet to start with, but you likely have tools that can then be expanded to include future work flows. Matter tracking can help with the broader challenge of keeping track of external suppliers (including legal spend), although many teams have now implemented a separate e-billing solution. Choosing a system often means you must compromise on what you show, but ideally, you want to cover:

- tracking the status of all internal and externally supported work (with enough data to allow for meaningful analysis of your processes),
- associated financial reporting on fees, and

[87] A Kanban board allows you to move cards (which can represent matters) between columns (representing stages), so you can see the status of each matter. A popular example of Kanban boards is Trello, but many platforms now have this capability.

- workflow to enable hand-offs between departments.

No system covers everything, and few teams have cracked the challenge of coordinating multiple systems. My advice is to accept that you may not have a single view for everything but try to keep to as few systems as possible and prioritise your most pressing needs.

Some systems already within your organisation may be helpful:

- **Ticketing systems**: Your IT department is likely to have a ticketing system for tracking IT issues and requests for help. You can repurpose these as a matter-tracking system.

- **Platforms**: You can use SharePoint and Power Automate in Office 365 to create simple workflows that are good enough to get going.

- **Business intelligence tools**: Business analysts in your organisation will probably be using analytics tools that you can repurpose for dashboards.

Document automation

Problem

How can you reduce the time it takes to create contracts from hours or even days to a few minutes while ensuring rigour and consistency?

Solution

Implement a document automation system and start an ongoing process to automate your contracts.

Points to consider

Document automation systems that let you create tailored documents based on the answers to questions are a must-have solution for several reasons:

- **Speed**: Creating a contract using document automation takes a few minutes. You can also create a suite of related documents at the same time, based on the same answers. The business can use document automation to generate simple contracts without needing to talk to legal.

- **Risk management**: Unfortunately, we all regularly make mistakes. Document automation removes many opportunities for error. Document automation also brings rigour to ensure the key issues are addressed in every contract, rather than relying on the user to remember them—it essentially acts as a checklist. It also helps ensure that your users don't use previous deal documents (with provisions negotiated out) for the next agreement.

- **Better contracts**: As issues come up, teams often keep adding points to contracts, and the templates rarely get shortened. There are also limits to how far you can expect a user to tailor a Word version of an agreement for a deal's circumstances. Document automation lets you break out of this cycle. You can tailor your contract each time to only include the relevant issues. The result is shorter documents that are faster to negotiate.

- **Iterative improvements**: Document automation helps you to continuously update your templates (rather than relying on epic redrafting projects). If you know that your users will use the latest version of the template through the system, it's easier to keep making changes to "knock the edges" off your contracts.

- **Happier business**: We've found that the crucial element in determining how business users feel about the contracting process is how quickly they can get going. If you give your business users the ability to create a draft safely using a document automation system, they get a near-instant result—an easy way to be a hero.

There are many document automation systems now on the market. Our favourite is Docassemble, a free and open-source system. If you want a more expensive commercial solution, you have quite a range to choose from: some are powerful and sophisticated, some are pretty and don't do much. As you evaluate the options, consider the following:

- **User interface**: The user interface matters a lot to the users. It needs to be easy to use, ideally to the point where little training is necessary. Beyond that test, beware of weighting eye candy over the other factors on this list.

- **Turning on/off language**: You may already have some simple document automation in your business that can only fill in blanks. These simpler systems don't allow for sections of the document to be turned on and off and cannot handle complex contracts. Make sure that your solution has this feature.

- **Editing**: A simple editing environment will be critical if you want your tech-minded team members to automate templates. Ask for a demo of how this part works and run like hell if it needs serious programmers to create templates. Think through in advance the kinds of customisation your documents are likely to need and ask the vendor to confirm that their system can handle the intricacies[88].

- **Integration**: It's becoming increasingly important to integrate document automation with other systems (through APIs[89]). You may want to get source data from other systems or send the document straight out through an e-signature system. It's worth checking what integrations exist[90].

- **Templates v clauses**: some systems are built around automating separate complete templates, others are built around clause libraries. The latter would seem to help with ensuring consistency across your different contracts, but my experience is that it can introduce new complexity in maintaining your templates. In particular, the context around the clause can change the wording used, so this approach can lead to clumsy drafting and unintended consequences if you change a clause used in multiple templates.

- **Browser v Word plugins**: Some contract management system vendors have created Word plugins to provide

---

[88] For a real test, ask the supplier whether their system can handle "repeats within repeats". For example, can the system allow the user to specify an arbitrary number of entities and for each entity specify an arbitrary number of attributes to appear in the contract (such as multiple companies and multiple director details for each of them)?

[89] API stands for "application programming interface", a way for one system to talk directly to another without needing to involve humans.

[90] If you are going to rely on the API, ask someone technical to review the API documentation. Effective APIs are notoriously hard to find in legal tech.

document automation capabilities. The browser-based systems tend to be much more powerful.

- **Hosting**: All legal tech now comes with a cloud option, and many of the newer ones are only cloud-based. Cloud-based systems will be faster to implement. Ensure you know at the beginning of the selection process whether your IT department will insist on only using systems hosted in their own data centres.

- **Licensing model**: Some suppliers charge a flat fee per organisation, some charge per end-user or document. Check that you aren't going to be accidentally paying a fortune for the system as usage grows.

- **Approvals**: Some of the systems offer additional functionality for adjacent parts of the contracting process, such as approvals. This can be helpful when a business user creates a document, but legal wants to check it before it goes out.

- **Analytics and reporting**: Some systems are better than others at tracking usage and allowing reporting. These reports can clarify where you have take-up of the system and identify opportunities for improvement.

Remember that choosing a system is the easy part. We will be covering the automation process in the Refinement chapters.

Case Study: Document Automation

A large technology company was looking for new ways of working that would streamline their contracting process to improve efficiency, make the best use of resources, and deliver meaningful impact to the broader business.

The company focused on high-volume, repetitive contracts with a value of less than a million pounds. Over three months, the company rewrote their most-used template, reducing it from 30 to 8 pages (and created a playbook).

The company automated the template and trained the business to use the tool to create the contracts themselves. The results were:

- an empowered business team with a streamlined workflow and without the previous bottlenecks,
- the company reduced the average time to close from months to a matter of days, and
- the in-house legal team could focus on more strategic work.

Case Study 6 - Document Automation

Word extensions[91]

Problem

How can you eliminate the inordinate amount of time spent fiddling with Word documents as part of the contracting process?

---

[91] Writing the second edition, I thought long and hard about whether to replace this section with the browser-based tools that are emerging for analysing contracts. I decided to keep it because (a) the browser-based tools tend to work best with the other side's paper and the objective is to be using your paper more often, (b) I have deep concerns about the quality of the output seen so far from many of these tools, and (c) we are kidding ourselves if we think we are about to escape Word and we have found these extensions to be invaluable when working in Word, which is a caustic environment for contracts.

Solution

Specialised extensions to Word can significantly improve the speed with which contracts can be reviewed and cost little compared to the time saved. They are also simple to install locally on your computer—a quick, easy win!

Points to consider

Word is a powerful tool, but it is generic and not designed to handle lawyers' issues. This can lead to unacceptable inefficiencies as lawyers struggle with documents and deal with broken formatting. Tools now exist that extend the scope of Word, adding functionality specially for lawyers. As examples of what these tools can do:

- generating issue lists from contracts,
- reversing track changes (so you can quickly and demonstrably reject a change),
- fixing broken documents at the press of a button,
- better document navigation, including being able to see pop-ups with definitions of capitalised terms,
- checking for missing definitions and other issues,
- cleaning up the track changes in documents (e.g., when your colleagues have all added their—conflicting—thoughts using their names), and
- a clause database, allowing lawyers to insert preferred language into contracts and collect useful clauses for the future.

These were the first software tools we built at Radiant Law as they provide such scope for saving time. We approximately halved the time it takes to review a mark-up using the tools we created. There are commercial products available that can save huge amounts of time fiddling with your contracts.

E-signatures

Problem

How can you speed up the signing process and guarantee you get a copy of the final signed agreement?

Solution

E-signatures are now one of the most common contracting technology solutions in use, so if you still haven't implemented them, do it right now.

Points to consider

Most countries have now recognised e-signatures as legally sufficient for most, if not all, commercial contracts (although not always for documents with more formal legal requirements, such as land transfers)[92].

E-signatures offer several advantages over wet ink:

- they are far more convenient, improving business satisfaction with the process,

---

[92] At their simplest, e-signature systems attach an image of a signature to a document and log the process of how it was signed (typically identifying the signer by a unique link sent to their email address). More complicated signing processes and technology can also be enabled for advanced and qualified electronic signatures under EU law.

- it is demonstrably faster to obtain signatures this way, reducing the time to close,
- the approvals process can be automated, making it easy to confirm that approvals were given,
- these systems help ensure that contracts are signed (no small feat), and
- they help you find your signed contracts and are also an excellent feed into a contract management system.

E-signature systems can also assist with the pre-signature approvals process, allowing you to send the finalised contract to the approvers (in a pre-set sequence if needed). You can also require them to consent before it is finally signed.

Contract management

Problem

How best to store your contracts and keep track of key dates and actions?

Solution

Put in place the most straightforward contract management system you can and be thoughtful about what data you need to track. In any case, try to avoid throwing away data that you have captured earlier in the process.

Points to consider

One of the most common refrains we hear from contracting teams is that they regularly can't find their signed contracts. Although there are many systems available to help with this (over a hundred), the problem can still arise when you have one. This is because collecting (and managing) contracts is fundamentally a process problem rather than a technology one.

Case Study: The New System

A chief procurement officer was frustrated that their team couldn't identify when the contracts in a particular category would be up for renewal. They installed a contract management system and had a review project carried out to populate the system. The total cost was over £3 million.

To justify the cost, the CPO mandated the collection of many data points for new contracts (not just renewal dates). Uploading a contract was so demanding that many agreements didn't get added by the procurement team. Other teams hadn't been consulted and ignored the system. As the records weren't complete, the procurement team had even more reason to avoid using the system. Renewal dates continued to be checked manually.

Case Study 7 - The New System

I recommend using as simple a system as possible, requiring only a minimal amount of information to be entered and relying on later data extraction exercises to answer future non-standard questions. I will discuss this further in Chapter 8.

For now, the data I would focus on collecting (apart from information on parties, renewal dates, and type) are:

- unusual long-term obligations on you (because you won't comply with them if they aren't made actionable), and

- changes to standard processes, such as approvals (so you know where there will be issues with later bulk updates across your agreements).

Bonus: GenAI

Problem

How best to learn where GenAI might help with your contracting?

Solution

Give your team access to GenAI and encourage them to experiment.

Points to consider

GenAI is being embedded in all of the IT systems we use. Licences can be expensive, and we are still in the early days of figuring out where it will add the most value. I gave a number of possible use cases in Chapter 5 and cautioned about some risks. It's quite possible that in a short time we will find ourselves in the trough of disillusionment[93] and attention will have moved on; my suspicion though is that the technology is here to stay and we will find use cases where it really does help.

This is the time to experiment, but as you do consider the following:

- **Confidentiality**: contracts can contain sensitive information, so keep an eye on the terms of use for the service you select and make sure that what you are uploading won't be used to train the system in a way that could later leak confidential information.

- **Hallucinations**: please don't ever trust the output, and train your team on the risks.

[93] From the Gartner Hype Cycle.

- **Sharing**: No one has yet fully cracked how best to use these new capabilities, so encourage your team to share what they have learned.

- **Other use cases**: our days are full of ambiguity and no one only works with contracts. Many of the best use cases may be in helping with other work.

Summary

The following are just the base systems you will want to put in place:

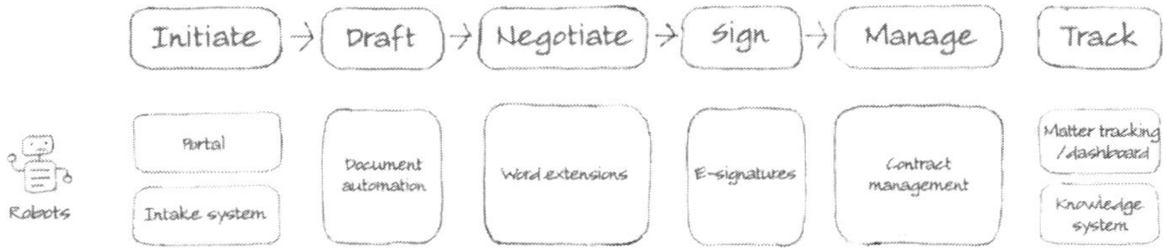

The systems you use will inevitably change over time; what matters is that you focus on adoption at each stage.

With the building blocks of processes, tools, and systems in place, next up is Refinement: the never-ending cycle of improving your contracting process.

Chapter 7 Refinement: Core Principles

For an industry that is so slow to move, the law has plenty of fashions. Year after year, proponents argue that a new approach can be applied and will change everything. Some of these ideas have left little trace (remember Big Data?), while others have helped. Regular practitioners of project management may have been surprised by the sudden enthusiasm for legal project management ("legal" is almost inevitably prepended) when the discipline is old and well understood in other quarters. Still, it's hard to argue that a little project management doesn't go a long way with running legal matters.

These external disciplines are discussed for a while in breathless terms and can be overwhelming to those who don't devote their lives to following the latest trends. Should one use Agile, Lean, Six Sigma, or even Lean Six Sigma? What about design thinking or even visually designed contracts? Where does data analytics, game theory, behavioural economics, or evolutionary psychology fit in? If you don't have a wall covered in Post-it notes, are you doing it all wrong?

How can you make sense of this all and get going? First, it is worth recognising that across many of these disciplines is a common thread: start with the customer's needs. Keep coming back to what matters to the stakeholders in your process ("customer" covers many of those involved or affected) and how you can better deliver it (otherwise known as creating value). Then you will be heading in the right direction. Second, it is better to choose one approach and stick with it than keep chasing novelty. Despite proponents arguing there is only one true way, these disciplines are more like the many faces of a single process improvement god. Third, don't worry too much about purity. If a tool from a different discipline looks helpful, use it.

At Radiant Law, we have adopted the Shingo Model across the firm, which is effectively codified Lean[94].

As we move now to the third stage of improving your contracting—Refinement—I'm going to explore how to think about quality in contracting, the critical steps in speeding up contracting, how to approach continuous improvement, and finally, how to use data to support your improvement activities. All of these will help you apply the disciplines of process improvement to contracting.

What does "good" look like?

"***There is nothing as practical as a good theory.***" – Kurt Lewin

What is absent from many contracting improvement programmes is a broad understanding of what good looks like. Instead, a particular problem is identified, a (usually overly complex) solution is devised, and off we go. However, to evaluate, prioritise, and move forwards thoughtfully, you need a big-picture perspective of where the strengths and weaknesses of your organisation's end-to-end contracting lie and which of them matter. To figure that out, you need a theory of contracting quality[95].

Although rare to find in the wild, the basics of a coherent approach to contracting quality are simple: Value lies in the eye of the

---

[94] For an excellent discussion of how different improvement approaches best apply to the maturity of products, see Simon Wardley's post: https://blog.gardeviance.org/2015/06/why-agile-lean-and-six-sigma-must-die.html. For more about the Shingo Model see https://shingo.org/shingo-model/

[95] See Professor Daniel Linna's essay on quality in law for a broader discussion of this topic: https://www.legaltechlever.com/wp-content/uploads/sites/151/2020/03/Linna-Evaluating-Legal-Services-Quality-Value-2020-03-12.pdf

beholder. There is no objective measure of value; it depends on what's needed by the person being asked. Quality is a function of how well what you deliver meets that person's needs. Therefore, you need to figure out who to ask, establish what they want, and then see how well you are doing against their expectations.

Who are your stakeholders?

Traditionally, if you were a forward-thinking organisation, you would say that the "customer" is the person whose opinion matters. This neat phrasing doesn't solve the problem if you are trying to improve the contracting process within your business:

- There is no one customer within your organisation—all businesses are complex, and there are lots of departments that will benefit in some way from your contracts.
- In this age of environmental, social and governance (ESG) concerns, we are moving to a broader perspective of stakeholders, which includes those participating in delivering the contracts and those impacted by the agreements in other ways.
- Given that the contracting process's purpose is to create sufficient confidence to launch a mutually beneficial commercial relationship, the other party must be a relevant stakeholder, too.

Therefore, contenders for your list of stakeholders should include at least the "business", legal, finance, sales, procurement, operations, subject matter experts, the contracting team itself, and the other side.

What matters to your stakeholders?

As well as many potential stakeholders, many things may matter to them. Broadly, however, there are three dimensions to consider:

- **Contracting process**: how well the contracting process itself is running.
- **Contract**: the quality of the final agreement produced by the contracting process.
- **Commercial relationship**: the quality of the relationship created, which builds on both the process and the contract.

Each of these three dimensions has multiple aspects that may be relevant to your stakeholders.

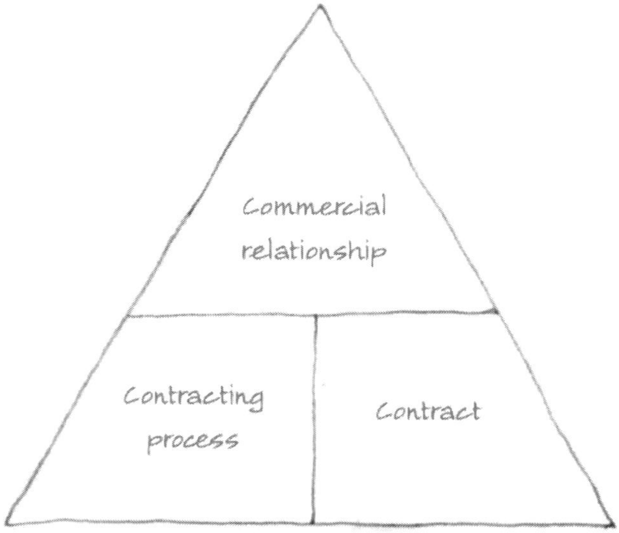

Figure 14 - Aspects of quality in contracting

Contracting process

- **Time to close:** How long does the end-to-end contracting process take[96]? We think this is one of the most important metrics of all.

- **Cost and efficiency**: How much does the contracting process cost for each contract supported? How much time does the team spend on each contract? Ideally, as little as possible, with recognition that it is inefficient to have multiple rounds of negotiations to close minor points.

- **Reliability and responsiveness**: How predictable is the process? How smooth is the process? Does the stakeholder know when they will get a response, and will it be quick? The time for requests to be acknowledged is often one of the most critical metrics for the business. We've identified strong correlations between customer satisfaction and this measure (which preferably should be just a few hours).

- **Assurance**: How good is the work product? Does it follow the playbook? Is advice helpful, clear, and to the point? Are you regularly giving key points away in order to close faster?

- **Empathy**: How did the stakeholder feel during the process? Were they heard? What was the tone of the emails they

[96] There is a balance to be struck here. Closing the wrong deals quickly is unhelpful. Rapidly sending out a piece of work that is incomplete or inaccurate introduces unnecessary risk and may often slow the overall process down. "***Quality is free***," observed Philip Crosby. When I say that the time to close is critical, that assumes a level of quality that is covered in several of the other factors. However, high levels of fiddling with the wording through the drafting and negotiation stages, while common, is not necessarily adding value or meaningful quality.

received? How flexible was the service to accommodate nuances? Did anyone pick up the phone and talk to them?

- **Compliance**: Was the correct process followed? Was the right information sent to the right person?

Contract

- **Clarity**: How understandable and precise is the contract? Does it avoid ambiguity?

- **Length**: How short is the contract? Does it cut to the chase and focus on what matters?[97]

- **Relevance**: How relevant is the contract to what the parties are trying to achieve? Does it cover what matters for what they are buying and selling?

- **Accuracy**: How accurately does the contract reflect the underlying bargain? Are the parties getting what they expected?

- **Usability**: How easy is it to navigate the contract? Can the stakeholder find what they are looking for quickly? Can they be sure that they are reading only relevant part of the contract covering a particular topic?

- **Legal application**: Does the contract appropriately take account of relevant laws to give effect to the parties' intention?

---

[97] Keeping the contract short makes it easier to digest and use. It can also impact time to close. One company tried an experiment of comparing the time to close of one- and two-page NDAs. The one-pager got signed on average in a day while the two-pager took a week.

- **Hygiene:** Is the contract free of typos and formatted consistently? Are the cross-references correct? Interestingly, we occasionally see this metric as the only quality measure in requests for managed legal services. It seems a bit trivial in the context of this list, but I suppose caring about the details is a reasonable proxy, at least to some degree, for caring more widely about the contract. Still, I think we can do better with what we measure.

Commercial relationship

- **Meets commercial objectives:** Has each party achieved its goals for the commercial relationship in the deal? Have the parties expanded the pie and gotten more than they hoped for?

- **Relationship alignment**: Is the relationship set up to succeed? Are the incentives aligned so it is in both parties' interests for the relationship to be long-term and mutually beneficial? Is there a strong likelihood that parties' objectives will be delivered? Is there room for the relationship to grow beyond initial expectations? Is the relationship well-positioned for possible future changes? Has the process created or reduced trust?

- **Risk handling**: Have risks been identified and addressed appropriately? Is the best party (usually the one with the most control of the outcome) bearing each risk? Has each party ensured that the contract does not pose a serious potential threat to them?

- **Profitability**: Is the contract profitable for both parties? For customers, this means that it will deliver more value than the price. For suppliers, it means the price paid exceeds the costs.

With these facets (or at least the ones that most matter to your stakeholders), you can generally measure how contracting is working by comparing the contracting process's performance against your desired standards. You can also measure on a per-contract basis how well the commercial relationship measures up to the ideal and to the contract itself, including how far the agreement deviates from the ideal represented by the standard terms. Finally, you can measure how a contract performs over its term, comparing the actual outcome to expectations.

Don't get bogged down in trying to be too accurate with your measurements. An educated opinion is good enough to get going (and maybe sufficient). Identify your stakeholders, talk them through the different facets described above, and get them to prioritise what is most important to them. Then ask them where the most significant gaps are between what they need and what they perceive is happening. Start your improvement activities by focusing on those gaps.

Closing contracts quickly

"Direction is more important than speed. You can go fast in the wrong direction." - Redfoo

Despite the quote (yes, get the contract right too), one of the most important metrics is time to close. What improvements will significantly impact speed?

Consider a typical negotiation process. I'm going to break it into blocks of, say, two to four weeks. Some stages will be faster in practice than others on any given deal, but the sequence is inevitable. Although we may all have experienced shorter times for any of these stages, we will also have experienced much longer.

Here is an archetypal negotiation process based on your paper:

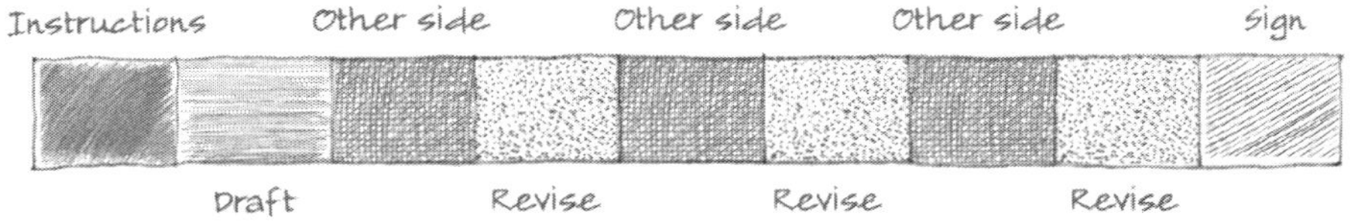

Figure 15 - Contract stages at the beginning

The stages are:

- **Instructions**: getting a clear understanding of what the business is trying to achieve with the contract.

- **Draft**: creating the first draft of the contract and getting the business sign-off.

- **Other side**: the other side reviews the contract and provides a mark-up.

- **Revise**: you, in turn, review the draft and provide your mark-up of the mark-up and so on.

- **Sign**: each party goes through its approval process and signs the agreement.

So, assuming a couple of weeks for each stage, little of which is spent on the deal, that comes to about a four-month end-to-end process. How can we shorten it?

By now, we know the three steps to reduce the timeframes:

- sort out the intake process using a form to elicit clear instructions that don't need further explanation,

- introduce document automation to create the contract in a matter of minutes, and
- use e-signatures to complete approvals and signing in a matter of hours.

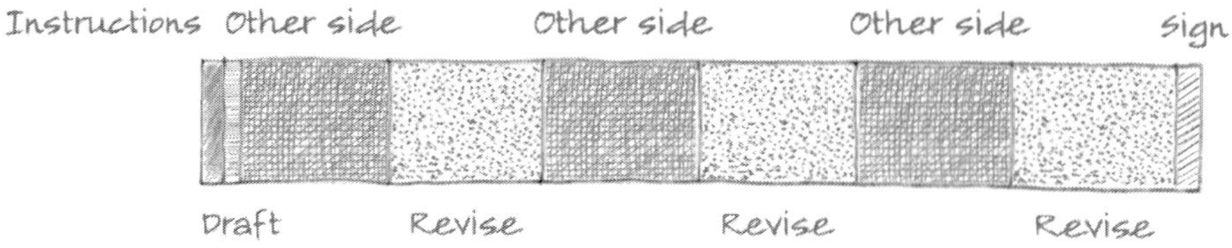

Figure 16 - Contract stages after initial improvements

Already, you've reduced the time to close by 30%. Good work! Next:

- Reduce the time it takes your team to review the contracts from two weeks to half a day. Think that's impossible? I'll explain how we did it at Radiant Law in a moment[98].

That will give you this picture, which is a total reduction of over 60%:

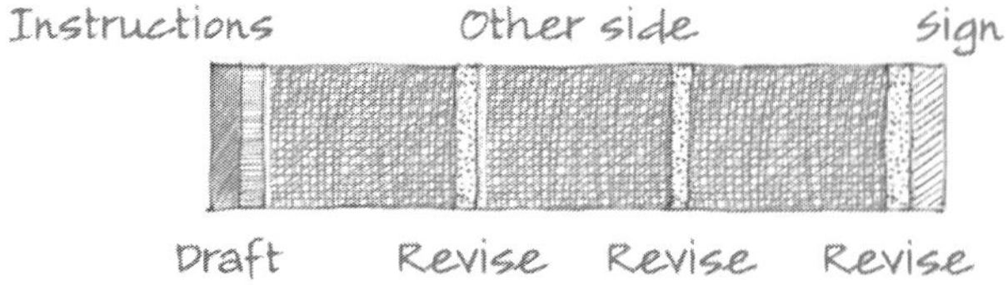

Figure 17 - Contract stages with faster turn-around times

[98] The market standard for managed legal services is currently a two-day turnaround. If you can't meet that internally for simpler standard contracts, it is perhaps time to consider using an external supplier (and focusing the internal team on value-creating strategic activities that cannot be outsourced).

Now it gets tricky. However efficiently you operate, you can't assume that the other side will get quicker[99].

So, the solution to get the next big time saving is to eliminate the other side's need to review the agreement more than once. What you are trying to achieve is a review resulting in no comments raised, and if there are comments, you deal with them effectively in your next round to conclude the deal. Ideally, the process would look like this:

Figure 18 - Contract stages with reasonable terms

And this is why it is so valuable to use reasonable standard terms (as well as ones that are short, clear, relevant, and well designed). Total time saved: about 85 %.

Another way of looking at this is to show the value-adding time versus the elapsed time in the initial version. The changes we have made have primarily removed waiting time as well as unnecessary back-and-forth communication:

[99] It's true that turning a draft around quickly can influence the other side's turnaround time; if you manage to get it back on the same day, they will remember what is happening and you may find that, in some cases, the contract is, in turn, sent back on the same day. But this effect is the exception in our experience. It's more likely that the agreement will go back on the pile unless it is particularly urgent.

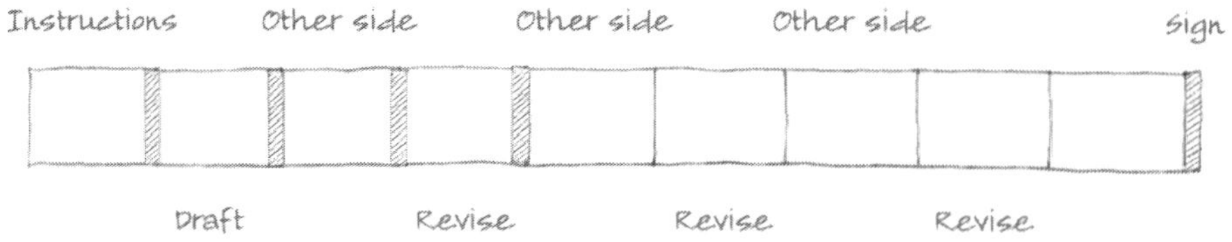

Figure 19 - Contract stages showing value-adding time

Using data

"In God we trust, all others must bring data." - W. Edwards Deming

As you improve your process, you're going to need data to understand what is happening, where to focus your improvement activities, and whether your "improvements" are improving things. Unfortunately, most companies have very little data about their contracting processes, and many don't even know how many contracts they sign each month.

As other departments have created dashboards and started to analyse, with increasing rigour, data related to their part of the business, legal has exhibited jealousy—if not a downright fear that it is falling behind. One of the biggest drivers of new technology projects for contracts is the desire to know when, for example, renewal dates are happening (contract management) or how many contracts are being negotiated (intake systems). The suppliers, noticing this need, have been quick to produce beautiful dashboards.

But the formula seems to be[100]:

1. Buy technology with a dashboard
2. Data!

[100] From South Park, of course. https://knowyourmeme.com/memes/profit

3. ????
4. Profit!!!

A few conceptual problems are going on here:

- Data by itself doesn't change anything. As Douglas Hubbard points out in his brilliant book ***How to Measure Anything***, the point of measuring is to make a good enough decision. You need to start first with the decision you want to make and what data is missing, rather than starting with the data someone else thinks matters.

- The kinds of data you get from a typical system with a dashboard will be initially informative (it would be nice to know how many contracts you are supporting). However, it will become less so over time as you make decisions informed by that data (although keeping your process under control will always be necessary).

- The data that most contracting technology can give you is limited. It may show you what is going on at a high level with your contracts, but over time, you will need granularity.

This doesn't mean that dashboards have no use. Used well, they can help you spot trends over time and exercise control by ensuring that the process is running smoothly[101] and reacting where things aren't working. However, the real value comes from a more purposeful approach to collecting and using data.

---

[101] Although that requires the process to be under "statistical control", and most aren't.

Keeping track

One approach to collecting data is to put in place technology using data from document automation, workflow, and the other systems we covered in the Robots stage. Systems-created data can give powerful insights into the contracting process, and we use this regularly at Radiant Law. The problem is that extracting, cleaning, and using this data can often require software development and data analytics skills that are not readily available to the average contracts team (although GenAI may help upskill the team).

As a starting point, informed estimates are not valueless. Polling the team for a quick answer can give you all sorts of insights. However, going beyond this, there is an approach to data that is so simple and effective that it's incredible that it's not more common: paper, pencil, and checkmarks.

If you want to know how many contracts you support a year, don't ask the team how many they support at any point in time. Not only is that not how you count, but it encourages your team not to close their contracts. Instead, track on a piece of paper how many come in over a few weeks or a month. Feels too inaccurate? Keep counting. Want to know what is slowing your team down? Ask them to write down the main obstacles on a piece of paper and then add a checkmark whenever one comes up. Want to know which points you are over-negotiating? Keep a list of clauses and add a checkmark when you negotiate it.

Likewise, by tracking the same issues after you've made a change, you'll be able to see how successful you've been at solving the problem. Overall metrics are essential, but they are often lagging indices. It is hard to show the impact of improvement exercises until much later. It's also hard to connect small changes to overall improvement metrics, meaning the effect could easily get lost in the noise. Using simple tracking exercises that are quick to perform and quick to show improvements allows you to move fast.

When you start measuring, one thing to bear in mind is Goodhart's Law[102]: When a metric becomes a target, it ceases to be a good measure. In other words, teams inevitably start optimising for the metric rather than the underlying goal. This phenomenon can lead to counter-productive behaviour[103].

A final thought when you start collecting data in systems: the SALI Alliance is doing terrific work creating standard taxonomies for the legal industry. It's free to use, will support interoperability between systems and possible future migrations, and it saves you from having to figure it all out yourself. If you can use SALI standards, please do.

Continuous improvement

I've argued for keeping transformation projects short and sweet. Once you've put the basics in place with the Repeatable and Robots stages, generally, you're going to want to focus on even smaller projects. We've had success with a couple of approaches to maintaining this momentum.

---

[102] Like Campbell's Law, which states that the more a quantitative social indicator is used for social decision-making, the more it will be subject to corruption pressures and the more apt it will be to distort and corrupt the social processes it is intended to monitor.

[103] To understand how bad this can get, read up on how the British colonial administration in India created a cottage industry of snake breeding when they offered to pay a reward for every cobra caught! https://en.wikipedia.org/wiki/Perverse_incentive

The first is a quarterly cycle of identifying key projects to deliver in consultation with the stakeholders. A quarter of a year works well. You can achieve a surprising amount in a quarter, but it's not so long that the project becomes irrelevant or forgotten. It also allows you to accommodate spikes in volume. We often find they happen at the end of the quarter, and it eventually sinks in with the team that the first month of each quarter is the time to crack on with continuous improvement rather than take a break after the end of the last quarter.

Quarterly projects work well when you know what you need to put in place, but you'll find that change becomes more ambiguous over time, as it is less clear what will work. We've found that the Lean approach of using management challenges works best.

An excellent explanation of this approach can be found in the ***Toyota Kata***[104] books by Mike Rothers, which are a good way to introduce Lean to your organisation.

The katas involve the leadership setting challenges that the organisation is going to meet by a particular date. The team members then need to figure out how to meet the challenge by identifying where they are (the current condition), where the next intermediate goal is (the target condition), and what obstacles stop them from achieving the target condition. As they work on removing the obstacles, the chosen metric will hopefully be improving. Once the target condition is met and becomes the current condition, a new target condition is set until the challenge is completed. This structured and empirical approach to change can

---

[104] The term "kata" comes from karate, where it refers to rote exercises for training muscle memory. The purpose of the katas (the improvement kata and the coaching kata) is making scientific thinking a natural instinct.

lead to dramatic improvements, as shown by the following case study.

Case Study: The Turnaround

At Radiant Law, we found that customer satisfaction was heavily driven by how fast we acknowledged the initial request for help from a business user. We were operating on a two-day service level for turning the work itself around (either drafting the contract or dealing with a mark-up back from the other side). We reviewed the time it took to complete the work, and it was clear that it was typically taking less than two hours.

We were comfortably meeting the two-day service level (the average was about a day and a half), but the deal was only being worked on for about 5 per cent of the time that it was with us. So, we set a six-month challenge for the team to reduce turnaround times to 75 per cent completed in half a day (we knew that there would always be outliers that would take longer).

To meet the challenge, the teams on each account tracked the actual performance of turnarounds weekly, reporting through our workflow platform. It turned out that we weren't measuring consistently or accurately enough to see the impact of our improvements, which we fixed with changes to our platform.

Once we had better data, we followed a weekly cycle of setting targets by account and experimenting with removing obstacles. We also redesigned the firm diary so that lawyers had set periods twice a day when they knew they had time to work on deals. By the target date, we had consistently brought down the time taken to turn deals around to meet the "75-per-cent-in-half-a-day" challenge.

This change had some interesting side effects. The team was less stressed because they completed their work on the same day, so they didn't go home at night worrying about what they had to do the next day. We also saw our net promoter score with our business customers rise from about 50 to a perfect 100 for the next three months. As expected, this tailed off a little as the business users got used to the new turnaround times, but it remained over 80, suggesting that speed matters a lot!

Case Study 8 - The Turnaround[105]

Summary

Although there are many process improvement approaches, they all come back to figuring out what matters to your stakeholders, identifying performance gaps, and fixing the issues, ideally with short, quick projects. Try to maintain momentum with steady improvements.

In this chapter, I explained the key steps you need to take to speed up contracting and how to collect data so you can identify key obstacles and confirm that your improvement activities are helping. Finally, I gave two models for improvement: quarterly projects and challenges.

With the basics covered, let's now look at how we can apply these approaches to contracting to solve the most pressing problems.

---

[105] Radiant Law now measures customer satisfaction as a score out of 5 and are running at 4.7 out of 5 from business users. The most common reason given is how quick we are, the next most common is how nice and helpful the team is to work with.

Chapter 8 Refinement: The Steps

Many of the Refinement activities are ongoing improvements, as there will always be things that can be improved. So, the Refinement stage never ends. The key activities are:

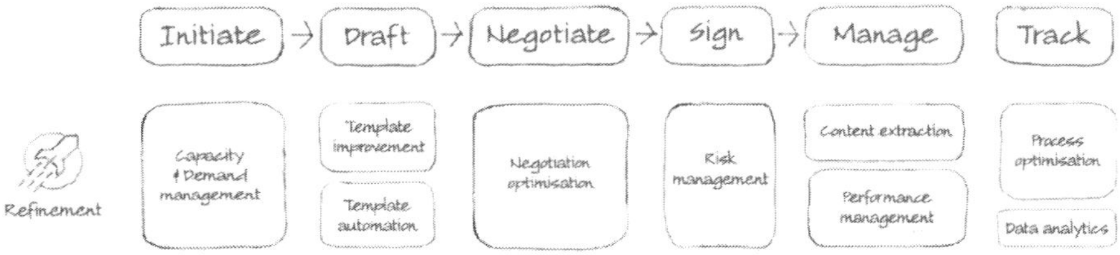

Figure 20 - Refinement stage steps

Talk to your stakeholders to find the gaps between their needs and reality, then start there.

Capacity and demand management

Problem

How to handle spikes in demand for contractual support without slowing everything down?

Solution

Rather than just allowing spikes to overwhelm you, reduce their frequency, severity, and impact and increase your ability to flex with demand.

Points to consider

Spikes in demand regularly swamp most teams, slowing down their ability to turn deals around.

There are several tactics that you can deploy to manage these spikes:

- **Prioritising deals**: We have seen great success in handling bottlenecks by having teams agree with business leads the contracts to prioritise, thus helping meet quarter-end targets.

- **Pricing urgency**: We've also seen teams agree on pricing with their suppliers based on the time taken to turn the work around. The business can choose whether they really need an expedited service. This is less relevant with Radiant Law, given our half day turnarounds as part of the base service.

- **Resource planning**: Get projections from the business on their expected sales and procurement activities and have a single shared plan for the team. Use this to balance resourcing with demand. Keep pushing the planning horizon out. Appoint members of your team to act as business relationship leads with your major customers in the business.

- **Build more scalable resourcing**: Supplement your internal team with third parties who can cost-effectively flex their available resources to handle spikes.

- **Increase self-service**: Run an ongoing programme to increase self-service, including giving business users access to document assembly to create their own simple agreements, as well as playbooks and other resources to handle more contracts.

- **Reduce batch processing**: It's easy to create bottlenecks that lead to unnecessary spikes in volume. These bottlenecks might be draft contracts left to fester on the sales team's desks until the end of the day on Friday or managers needing to give approvals. A quiet word with regular culprits may help; if not, cap the amount of work in progress that will be accepted at one time and make it clear what caused the resulting delays.

- **Reduce the work needed to support an agreement**: Many of this book's suggestions reduce the time and effort required to support contracts. The impact will be increased productivity.

Template improvement and negotiation optimisation

Problem

How to minimise the number of rounds of negotiations?

Solution

In Chapter 7, I explained that reducing the number of rounds of negotiations is critical to reducing the time to close. You need to minimise unnecessary contentious points by refining your templates and playbooks.

Points to consider

People can be just plain difficult. Whether it's a one-off lousy day or a lifetime of grumpiness, you're going to receive unreasonable responses to the most reasonable of terms. In our experience, if you can get this down to less than 10% of the time, so be it.

What's in play is how the other 90% of companies react to your standard terms. To get rid of rounds of negotiations, you need to be sending out agreements and taking negotiation positions that encourage closing rather than trench warfare.

While you will hopefully have made significant progress with this in the Repeatable stage, you're still likely to be surprised at what people misunderstand or react to in practice. That's OK. You just need to keep improving the draft. Similarly, you will have created a playbook in the Repeatable stage, but are the positions you're taking helping to close the contract or extending negotiations unnecessarily?

As you think about how far you want to go with refining your terms and negotiation positions, let's consider the perennial question of whether it's worth throwing in points to concede later.

To answer this, imagine who is going to be reviewing your contract. These days, it's usually an in-house lawyer. This lawyer inevitably has other things to do. Your deal is probably not at the top of their list of priorities, and they're not going to get much recognition for working late. In other words, they have better things to do than have multiple rounds of negotiations. They're going to read your draft (or changes) looking to agree, and the chances are that only when they find a point worth reacting to will they start marking up. So why give them a reason to make changes? Focus instead on knocking all the edges off so that they don't have to change anything. While you're at it, make sure that you have covered sufficiently the regulatory and other issues that subject matter experts on the other side can be so picky about.

If you need a way of dealing with a negotiator who raises a lot of unreasonable points, don't trade; just say no, explain the issues and hold the line.

With that in mind, here are some points on making ongoing improvements to templates and playbooks:

- **Make regular changes:** Rather than treating playbook or template improvements as a one-off event, make changes at least every few months.

- **Track the frequency of points:** We've built sophisticated software for identifying the issues that come up in negotiations across many drafts, but you don't need this to get started. Just keep a list of the main points and track those that come up. Prioritise the most frequent issues.

- **Removing issues beats collecting fallbacks**: It's better to get rid of a point altogether than have a fallback position in a playbook that you have no problem with conceding. If you can get rid of the issue, then just do it. Both terms and playbooks should be getting shorter as you get smarter.

- **Make it soothing**: A law firm partner I used to work for once said to me: "the purpose of a contract is to send the other side to sleep." It is a little too cynical for my taste, but it makes an essential point about how the wording of a clause can make all the difference between regular fights and nary a mention. If you can't get rid of issues, see if you can make them more palatable. If the point is a must-have but causes regular fights, then perhaps get ahead of the conversation by sending an explanation with your first draft. While you're at it, try to design the contract to make it as accessible as possible to head off issues.

Template automation

Problem

How to get your contracts automated?

Solution

Set your legal experts to work with an automation expert and get something simple up and running as quickly as possible.

Points to consider

So now you've got a shiny new document automation system courtesy of the Robots stage. Will it become another example of "shelfware", or are you going to use it?

You were probably told the system would make it easy for lawyers to automate their documents. The reality is that few, if any, team members will have the temperament or interest to climb the learning curve, start automating, and then keep going with creating automated templates. Without automated templates, no one can use the system to create new agreements. With that in mind, here are some key questions.

Who is going to do the actual automation?

To automate, you need legal expertise in the subject matter and technical expertise in the system. Ideally, this would be one person. But the reality is that systems are too complex for you to assume that every lawyer will learn to automate their documents.

The best outcome in practice is for a legal expert (who understands enough about the system) to work with a technical expert (who understands enough about contracts). The more legal background the technical expert has, the better, but people combining deep skills in both are unicorns (well, one or two exist).

As an organisation trying to automate your contracts, you have two options. The first is finding someone tech-savvy, interested in learning, and who has the time. Get them to work with the technical expert and learn. This approach can work, but progress may be plodding if your team members do this as a side project. The alternative is to bring in a third party. This will usually be a lot faster, but you need to factor this into your budget and bear in mind that there will be a need for ongoing support.

Which templates should you automate?

There are a couple of approaches to choosing where to start with automating your contracts:

- **Most common first**: Choose the most common contracts that you create as the first to automate. If they are complex, get the team at least partway there with the first draft. If they are simple, aim for completeness (at least for standard options).

- **Champion first:** Your team will inevitably have a range of opinions, from enthusiastic to deeply sceptical, about bringing in new-fangled technologies like document automation[106]. Finding an enthusiast who identifies opportunities for their benefit and then using the results to convince others is a well-tested route to bringing your team along with you. Your champion may be elsewhere in the business, so consider looking beyond the contracting team and think about how you will incentivise them.

How to approach automation?

Let's assume that the automation is going to be done by someone other than the contract expert. Otherwise, the steps below will be more straightforward:

---

[106] Invented in the 1980s.

- **Get your template**: You need to have a stable template before you can automate.

- **Flag the clauses that are optional and the variables**: This can be as simple as square bracketing the relevant provisions and adding a comment to show which row of the table below applies. Variables (e.g., party name) just need to be flagged with a comment once.

- **Create a table of questions**: Create a numbered table that sets out the questions and explanatory text (which will be an important part of guiding users and making the system more useable). Use comments or notes in the templates to link the questions to the relevant part of the template.

- **Automate the contract**: With the information above, the person doing the automation should have most of what they need to complete the work, bar some clarifications.

- **Test**: Back to the lawyer to test the template. It's not practical to try every possible combination, but I recommend the following steps:

  - walk through the questions and make sure that the right questions appear and the order is logical,

  - compare the output (with one set of options) against the original template to make sure that it looks right,

  - once you've confirmed that version, create a few other outcomes with the most significant structural differences to the first version, then run comparisons to do a sanity check, and

  - test the questions with someone else—ask them to create a document, then watch what they do and where they struggle. However simple you think you've made the questions, this will inevitably throw up surprising issues that you can fix quickly[107].

- **Launch**: Once you're happy with the output (and this process should take a week or two, not months), get your users to start using the system and have a single point for them to raise queries and suggestions.

- **Keep iterating (and keep adding templates)**: Get into a rhythm of looking at points coming up in negotiations that you can avoid by changing the drafting. Run a campaign to add more documents for automation based on successes to date.

I highly recommend getting a template up and running as quickly as possible and improving it over time. Think of your threshold as the absolute minimum number of questions and options to make the system marginally faster and more practical than manual drafting. Avoid disappearing down rabbit holes trying to cover every possibility. The law of diminishing returns applies, and you will identify the most useful additional options once you start to use the automated template.

One final thought on document automation: it is worth considering whether you always want to have more contracts put in place faster, especially before you put the technology in the hands of your business. For example, are you sure that your organisation will be better off signing more NDAs? If they really do, can you adopt a

---

[107] For more on user testing, see Steve Krug's excellent book ***Rocket Surgery Made Easy.***

standard (such as OneNDA or Bonterms)? As ever, unpack the problem before rushing to automation.

Contract risk management

Problem

How can you appropriately handle the risks associated with your agreement?

Solution

Consider how to manage threats and opportunities across the lifecycle of your contracts. We covered the basics in Chapter 4. Now you need to integrate across the following stages:

- intake, to ensure that you triage matters and identify and address risks early in the process,

- templates, to ensure that the focus is on the essential issues by type of contract and risk handling is balanced,

- negotiations, by refining the playbook to address significant threats appropriately and escalate to senior or specialist input at the right points,

- approvals and signing, with an updated risk review and a process to pass on knowledge of known risks to the contract management team, and

- after signing, so you actively manage the material risks within your control.

Points to consider

The traditional approach to risk management in contracting is to include as many protections as possible for potential threats while jumping on the other side's attempts to transfer risk back. Funnily enough, this mutually-assured destruction approach leads to slow negotiations and frequent stalemates without necessarily focusing on the real issues (as shown by the WorldCC surveys). Uncertainty is an inevitable part of day-to-day business life, and risk allocation is a more complex topic than just avoiding threats at all costs.

Let's define risk widely as significant uncertainty about both threats and opportunities. The goal in handling risk should be to identify those opportunities and threats, reduce uncertainty and apply mitigations where possible, and ensure that the appropriate party carries the consequences (up or down). It is not just about negotiating like Attila the Hun. Importantly, risk-handling doesn't end with signing, and material risks should be actively managed over the term.

I discuss both balancing negotiations and performance management in other sections in this chapter. Here, I'm going to focus on risk analyses.

A formal risk analysis can play an essential role in the process, and you shouldn't wait to start until the end of the deal. As you formalise your approach:

- create a checklist of issues to consider, which should go beyond just "legal" risks to include key commercial points (see Chapter 4 for the basics),
- focus in reports on essential topics and avoid minor points drowning them out,

- consider an insurance-style model of ***likelihood*** times ***expected impact*** when deciding whether an issue matters (yes, black swan events happen, but does the likelihood justify fighting the point?)[108], and

- try to avoid box-ticking exercises—getting this right requires real thought.

Performance management

Problem

How to make sure that you get the hoped-for value from your contracts?

Solution

Identify the critical points for performance management, including risks, put one or more people in charge of managing the contract, and treat your contract as a living document.

Points to consider

Interestingly, commercial contracts work, although they are rarely litigated. Parties seem to moderate their behaviours despite the low risk of being sued (it's such an expensive remedy that it's seldom worth pursuing) and generally comply with their obligations (though there are legions of minor technical breaches), so contracts kind of work[109].

---

[108] Consider your historical experiences when evaluating likelihood and see Douglas Hubbard's book ***The Failure of Risk Management*** for how to do risk analysis right with a probabilistic model.

[109] An explanation for this perhaps lies in Professor Macneil's identification of social norms as a crucial part of the framework within which contracts operate.

What's also interesting is the study by WorldCC mentioned in Chapter 1, which suggests that companies leak, on average, almost 9% of their hoped for value. Bad contracts rarely explode; instead, they may slowly bleed value due to poor scoping and pricing or drift from the original intentions.

Perfect value maximisation may never really be achievable. Still, I'm sure that we can always be better at managing and growing our commercial relationships[110]. We can certainly be better at managing contractual performance.

Rather than assuming that the things you care about in the contract will happen, you should actively manage the material opportunities and threats and track outcomes against initial expectations.

Pragmatically, it is best to focus on material agreements. Your process should include:

- identifying one or more people to take responsibility for managing the contract,
- a hand-over process after signature to pass the main identified risks to the contract owners (this is where it often goes wrong), and
- an oversight and reporting process.

You can track points in a spreadsheet in the first instance, but some contract management systems specialise in supporting more active management of large deals.

---

[110] 20% of companies are actively managing their commercial contracts, according to the Radiant Law Contract Scorecard.

You also need to manage the relationship itself. This entails more than mechanically attending governance meetings. It means getting ahead of nagging issues, identifying ways to improve both parties' outcomes, and working together to find opportunities to grow.

As you do this, it would help if you found a middle path between whacking your partner over the head with the contract and leaving it in a drawer. Avoid treating the contract as frozen in aspic for all time. It should move from a baseline for the start of the relationship to an ongoing record of the current deal, meaning that you continue to update it as a living document.

As you update your contracts, you'll find that keeping a final Word version from the point of signature is invaluable. You will also find that amending a contract with separate amendments, rather than continuing to update the final Word version, will quickly become unworkable.

Content extraction and contract data

Problem

How to store data relating to your contracts?

Solution

Design a data structure that makes sense, keeps data points from throughout the contracting process and the final versions of the contract, and minimises metadata.

Points to consider

I mentioned in Chapter 6 that finding your contracts was a process problem rather than a technical one. A simple solution to finding your contracts is to set up an email address to send them to after signature. If you can't make that work, a contract management system won't solve your problem finding agreements. E-signature systems help, but they too have to be used.

In the case study of the contract management system, we saw that requiring lots of data to be entered will probably reduce use. As tempting as it may be to capture everything, it will likely be counter-productive. So, keep the data fields to a minimum, but don't throw away any data you have. For the data to help, you will need a sensible way of storing it, so it's worth taking the time to think through the data structure. As noted in the performance management section, keep the final Word version. It will make future amendments much easier.

Not capturing every data point may appear unambitious, but future questions are surprisingly unpredictable, however much data you capture. Better to avoid manual extraction until it is needed. AI extraction is only going to get better, so future exercises will become easier with time.

Summary

Congratulations, you've made it through all the steps. It may feel like there is an insurmountable amount of work involved, but it can be done steadily and in bite-sized chunks. We've covered all of these steps in two chapters:

Of course, contracting is not staying still. In the next chapter, I will cover where the future of contracting seems to be heading. Please don't use future possibilities as an excuse to skip the steps in this book. All of these will still hold, and the future of contracting needs to be built on solid basics.

Chapter 9 Resourcing Contracting

Through this book, I've explored how to improve contracting as if your team is doing all the work. But as I alluded to in chapter 3, you don't have to do everything yourself, and there are good reasons to outsource at least part of the work.

In this chapter I'm going to cover:

- how to analyse your organisation's contracts by dividing them into four categories,
- the options you have for how each category of contracts can be supported, both internal and external,
- how the support model will hopefully change over time, and
- some of the objections that you are likely to hear as you review your approach to contracting.

Analysing your contracts

Optimal resourcing will depend on the type of contract. To figure out who should work on your contracts, start by categorising them on two different dimensions:

- How common are they? Are you dealing with many every day or are they a relative rarity?
- How risky are they? Are they high-value, high-complexity, and high-risk (these tend to go together), or are they well understood with manageable risks?

To be clear on the risk point—we are talking about the extent to which the deal is likely to be unusual and may need bespoke structuring. If your standard terms always exclude or sufficiently limit the key risks and the objective is to ensure those provisions don't materially change, then that is a low risk contract for these purposes. Such contracts need to be handled reliably, though, which is why common low risk contracts benefit so much from rigour and process.

With these dimensions you can create a two-by-two grid to start to sort your different contract types:

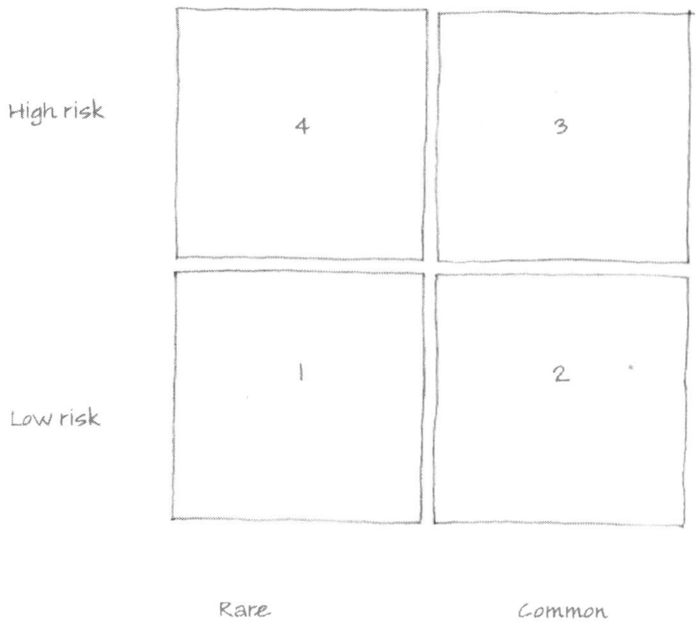

Figure 21 - Categorising your contracts

Of course, these dimensions are really spectrums, but forcing each contract type into one category can shine a light on what matters:

1. **Rare and Low Risk**: these contracts don't need material legal support. You can spot these contracts with triage, typically

looking for the characteristics I listed in chapter 4. This category can also include deal types (such as NDAs) where legal has provided standard forms and the other party isn't requesting changes—we'll come back to this later.

2. **Rare and High Risk**: this category is the reverse. The contracts really matter, but because they are rare it is not worth building internal expertise in your legal team.

3. **Common and High Risk**: these deals are key to delivering your organisation's strategy and are likely to have high business focus. Because of the regularity that they occur, their importance, and their tendency to involve working closely with the business, it's worth building expertise to handle these internally.

4. **Common and Low Risk**: these contracts also matter to your business. They will be the highest volume of your core contracts and fundamental to accelerating sales and procurement, but the lower risk means that they are easier to hand off. These are also the contract types that will benefit the most from applying lean processes and technology. Typical parameters for these contract types are:

- more than 50 contracts of a similar type a year,
- the value of the typical contract is less than £1-10m, what is "large" will tend to be proportionate to the size of your organisation, and
- the contracts are regularly negotiated, so not consumer contracts.

The two-by-two grid is for categorisation, but doesn't give the full picture on either volume or total deal value (across all deals), but when you categorise your contracts it will likely look like something like this for volumes:

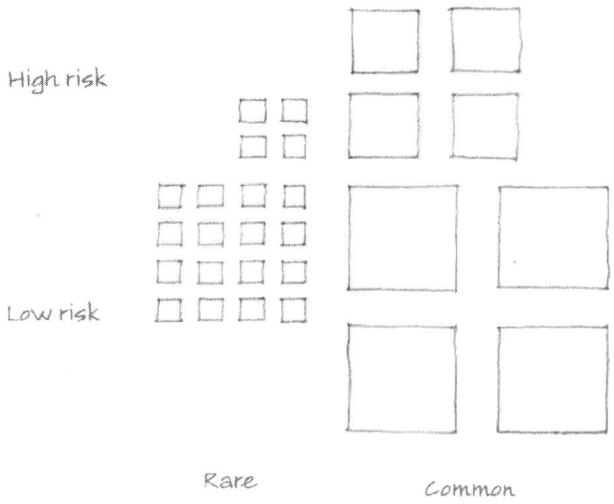

Figure 22 - Deal volumes by category

In other words, most of the volume is in the common and low risk deals. When looking at total deal values, the higher risk deals are going to tend to be far higher value, so the traditional pyramid for showing the breakdown evens out to some extent:

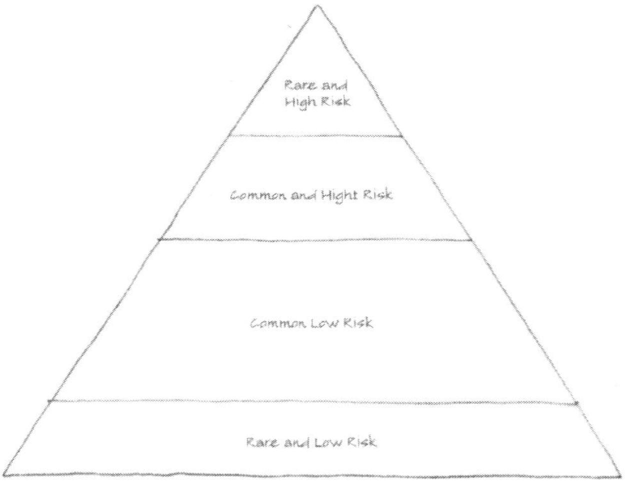

Figure 23 - Deal values by category

With these categories in mind, how might you support your different types of contracts?

Support options

You have options, perhaps more than you realise.

In-house: legal teams

In-house legal teams will be familiar to the reader, but a few observations. In-house legal teams now employ about a third of the legal profession. Their spectacular growth has been driven by a simple observation: if you have enough work to keep an in-house lawyer busy, they are a lot cheaper—about a third of the cost of using a law firm.

Cost may have driven the growth in in-house teams, but that misses the real value. In-house lawyers work far closer to the business, and can develop a far better understanding of the organisation's objectives and drivers, than an external lawyer. When in-house teams play to this advantage, they can add unique and deep business value.

Going further, in-house lawyers are better placed to handle ambiguity and make the more complex calls. Legal judgement adds huge value when wielded well, and in-house lawyers are able and often best-placed to take a view, especially as they represent the organisation, in situations where external suppliers may feel they need to defer.

In-house legal teams typically spend over 50% of their time dealing with contracts and are the default answer for contract support in enterprises. However, going back to the routine-to-innovative knowledge work model in Chapter 3, there is a big difference in practice between an in-house experienced deal lawyer leading high-end deals and an in-house junior lawyer working on simpler deals. The difference isn't just the experience of the lawyer, it's the nature of how routine you can make the deals.

Complex deals benefit most from experience, simple deals benefit most from process and tools:

- An experienced in-housed lawyer can handle a complex deal they are familiar with as well as any external lawyer.

- A junior in-house lawyer supporting simpler deals without a structure will rarely operate as well as an external junior lawyer working within a well refined-process and supported by technology and knowledge assets.

- In fact, a senior lawyer, whether internal or external, who is making it up as they go along, will be consistently beaten by a junior lawyer operating within a smart system (in the broad sense) when it comes to simpler, repeatable deals.

Which takes us to a fundamental problem faced by in-house lawyers: they are too often operating in an environment light on the process and technology I've described in this book.

In-house contract teams may sometimes be supplemented by "talent agencies" that can provide lawyers for a fixed period. This is more expensive than hiring, but neatly addresses challenges such as parental leave. I am bundling these providers into legal teams because, at the end of the day, you are receiving a no-doubt talented lawyer to join the legal team who is, ideally, expected to work in the same way as the rest of the team.

In-house contract teams need not, however, be locally-qualified lawyers. There are two other internal groups that might support your contracting: contract managers and service-centre teams.

In-house: contract managers

It's not entirely clear why lawyers have so effectively monopolised contracting. There isn't that much law involved in negotiating contracts, and what there is can of course be learned without needing full legal qualifications. Indeed, contracts classes at universities rarely teach much that is particularly relevant to real world contracting—we all learned how to do it on the job.

Despite the occasional snobbishness about legal qualifications, there are lots of excellent contract managers (championed by the wonderful WorldCC) supporting contracts in enterprises. That being said, a contract manager will tend to be paid less than a similarly experienced lawyer, so the cost differential can make this option attractive.

In-house: shared service centres

Another twist is a shared service centre, a way an enterprise can locate an internal contracts team in a lower-cost region (whether near-shore or off-shore). Many large organisations have already set up service centres to perform other back-office functions; some companies then bootstrap a contract management team to share this infrastructure, often staffed with locally qualified lawyers and contract managers.

This is another labour arbitrage play (note that everything in this section so far has been at least partly motivated by reducing the cost of the people doing the work). The problem with labour arbitrage is that it only gets you so far. When you have moved all of your work to the lowest-cost region on the planet, what do you do next? It's not as if cost pressures are going away.

This takes us to the other key point about shared service centres. The act of moving a service to a new team forces companies to start to formalise how contracting should be done. This is the perfect moment to implement the 3Rs methodology, but alas these centres can often in practice be seen as not only lower cost, but also lower quality, because the companies haven't followed through in investing in optimising how they do their contracting. And as I observed above, optimisation is most critical with the common and lower risk contracts that get sent to these centres. Which takes us to legal operations.

In-house: legal operations

An important new group has emerged within in-house teams: legal operations. Team members may range from lawyers who wanted to do something different; professionals hired from outside the legal industry who bring technology, finance, strategy, knowledge management, project management, process improvement, and/or data skills; and, let's be honest, one or two examples of administrators with new titles.

Legal operations are an important development, not because they are going to start delivering your contracts (that's the antithesis of their job description), but because at their best, they bring a super-power of accelerating the rest of your contracting team. Their impact may have been exaggerated a little at first (like so many fads in legal) but this group is adding more and more value.

A challenge legal operations faces is the ability to influence the team members doing the day-to-day contract work, and it can be particularly hard for "non-lawyers" (ghastly term) to take lawyers on a journey towards the light.

A far bigger issue, though, is whether improvement activities can and should be separated from the team doing the work. Fixing contracting requires a deep understanding of both contracting itself and disciplines outside the normal ambits of legal studies (see the skills the external professionals bring). If improvement is treated as a separate activity that is left to "the professionals", rather than the team at the coal-face, the chances of improving the right things is slim. This may explain a lot about the realities of enterprise contracting even after the arrival of legal operations.

External: traditional law firms

Law firms used to support most of the contracts that are now supported by in-house teams. Although companies then hired the same lawyers directly to save money, it's amazing how many smaller contracts are still being sent to traditional law firms. To give you a peak at where this chapter is going, we were recently brought in to support contracts in place of a traditional law firm, and our fixed pricing was about 10% of their cost with no assumptions.

Traditional law firms are still going from strength to strength for good reasons:

- they have deep expertise in rare, complex, and high risk deals, where it makes no sense to build an internal capability,
- they are easy to buy—you don't even have to come up with a detailed scope, just point them in the right direction and let the billable hours start being racked up,
- for the highest profile deals, you won't be fired for hiring a top firm, and
- every in-house team has at least one law firm on tap that has had a long relationship with their company.

For bet-the-company deals, traditional law firms will always be used, but there are challenges with using them for other categories, and it's not just the cost:

- even if they are charging on a fixed-price basis (which is still sadly not the norm), traditional law firms have the billable hour hard-wired in, so they tend to treat everything as bespoke,
- traditional law firms are also run by partners who are generally allowed to do things their own way, another reason why firms find it well-nigh impossible to implement a standardised approach to processes, and
- the billable hour-mentality also means that any technology that materially speeds up work will tend to be ignored (ask your favourite firm how many contracts they create with document automation).

So while traditional law firms may be excellent for rare and complex deals (remember we said that experience is most important for high complexity contracting), they are not only expensive but also slow for simpler deals. Earlier I said that turning a simpler contract in no more than two days is the target. A traditional law firm may easily take that long just completing the conflicts check.

In-house: the business

I didn't give the full picture when I said that contracts used to be supported by traditional law firms. In the beginning, the business teams were happily doing deals as they saw fit. This continued until someone at their company made a rule that contracts had to be checked by lawyers, usually because some contracting disaster had occurred, and only then were contracts sent in bulk to traditional law firms.

The rules requiring legal review generally only strengthened as legal departments grew. The new guardians of the company had to check everything, of course, and then the pile of contracts in front of the guardians started to grow.

The business teams may not, generally, be fully cognisant of the finer details of force majeure clauses, but they do have a major advantage: they are cutting the commercials and understand what they are trying to achieve with their commercial relationship. It's not ridiculous for them to handle contracts, with a few guardrails and tools, where:

- the nuances of force majeure clauses etc don't matter so much, and
- the contracts team hasn't built a slick standard support model.

If you check back to where I defined thresholds for rarer low-risk contracts in Chapter 4, you will see how you might determine when it is appropriate for the business to just get on with it.

In conclusion:

- there are more than just lawyers working on contracts internally,
- experienced in-house lawyers are great for regular, complex deals,
- labour arbitrage will only get you so far for your common, simpler contracts, and
- succeeding with common, simpler contracts requires taking process improvements and technology seriously, which in-house teams have generally been light on to date.

This all suggests that building an internal pyramid model with lots of lower-paid junior lawyers is not enough to meet the challenges.

Meanwhile, companies are still using traditional law firms, where in-house lawyers learned their trade (and the pyramid model).

External: alternative legal service providers (ALSPs)

This brings us to the ALSPs like Radiant Law. ALSPs are generally bringing two things to the table as a managed legal service for contracting:

- scalable access to lower cost regions, similar to internal shared service centres, and
- far better processes and technology.

In other words, ALSPs at their best provide a system (in the broad sense) within which their lawyers work, delivering better results for common lower risk contacts than an in-house lawyer could deliver without a system. Some ALSPs admittedly are just labour arbitrage plays but what you should be looking for is the system. As an example of what a good system can deliver, let's look again at turn-around times. ALSPs should be hitting two days (Radiant Law is 4 hours), the average in-house team is taking on average 30 days (or 11 days in the top quartile). You can see the difference a system brings.

There are other advantages to using an ALSP:

- They bring experience on both process and content from other accounts, meaning that you get best practices out of the box.
- You get real-time data so a much better understanding of what is happening and more control.
- Everything should be fixed price, based on outputs, such as a fixed price per contract. If you are paying per lawyer for an ALSP then you are definitely doing it wrong and are not buying a system (or true scalability and efficiency).
- You get access to specialist skills such as automation and data analytics as part of the service.
- You get technology embedded within the service, saving you from having to do your own technology projects, with all the associated cost and risk.
- Everything keeps getting better, with integrated continuous improvement.

It's hard to compete with specialists, so if there is enough volume to justify the service then ALSPs are an excellent option for simpler higher volume contracts.

ALSPs are not the right solution for every company. You need sufficient volume and if your contracts are inherently highly variable, not just because they are currently being done in an ad hoc way, then you may be better off with an in-house team.

External: consultants

Finally, if you want to transform an internal team then there are companies that will work with you to support activities like technology implementations. This is a good way to add skills that may be missing in your team, but make sure you budget for future changes.

Radiant Law used to do this as a stand-alone service, but we stopped when it became clear that the value we could add was less than delivering a managed legal service that keeps getting better. However, there is excellent support out there if you need it.

Resourcing your contracting

Let's go back to the diagram at the beginning of this chapter and fill in the squares on who is best to support each category of contracts:

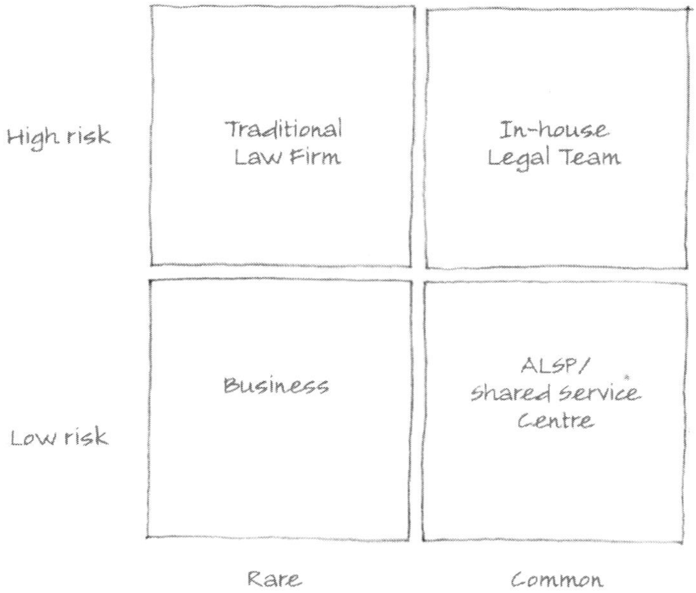

Figure 24 - Resourcing - Stage I

This is what we are seeing the most advanced large companies doing. For smaller companies, as I observed above, the bottom-right box may also be an in-house team if there isn't sufficient volume of similar contracts. The best practices in this book will still very much apply to that box.

For the companies that have adopted this model, it then tends to evolve over time as their contracting approach becomes more sophisticated:

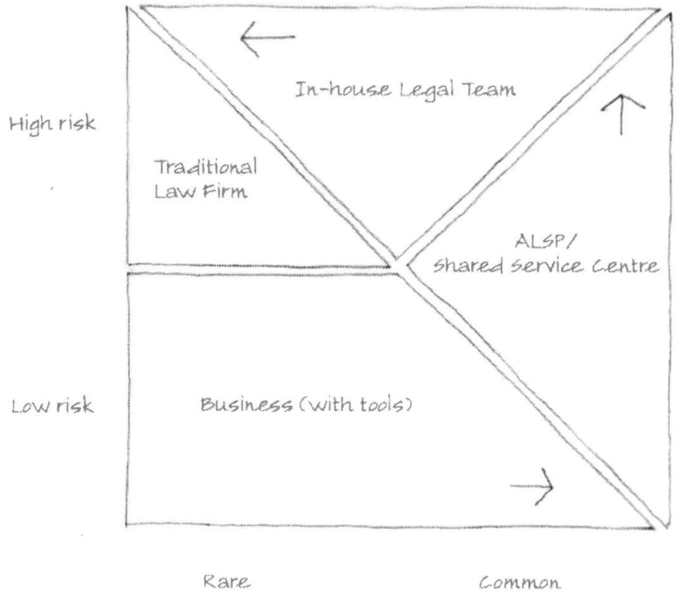

Figure 25 - Resourcing - Stage II

A few things are going on in the picture above:

- We have extended the role of the business. In the same spirit as doing your own shopping checkout, we want to increase self-service in the business by giving it the tools to safely handle more by itself.

- The managed legal services provider or shared service centre should, over time, be taking on more complex work as part of "taming" additional types of contracts.

- In turn, the in-house team should be upskilling to become capable of handling more of the work that would otherwise be sent to law firms. This instantly delivers additional cost savings and makes their roles more engaging.

- The law firms' role reduces over time. While there will always be a need for specialist advice on the hardest of deals, most law firms are too busy pricing themselves out of the market to be used more generally.

The overall impact of this evolution is a significant reduction in the total cost of support, with a greater emphasis on technology, self-service, and codified knowledge, in addition to an upskilled in-house team focused on more stimulating work.

The trick, of course, is not to see this as just a way to move the cost from one budget (legal) to another (business). Your goal is to reduce the activities required to support the more straightforward contracts. Expensive senior resources can transfer some of their responsibilities to more empowered juniors, allowing them to work on the more complex transactions and challenges the business faces and an ALSP can help with this too.

But what about...

"An objection is not a rejection; it is simply a request for more information." - Bo Bennett

I've described in this book how to rethink how contracting is performed and I've given options in this chapter about who supports it for different types of contracts. All of this is a message of change, and let's face it, humans only like change when it's happening to someone else.

Whichever paths you take to change how you support your contracts, there are objections that you will likely hear. Let me address a few of the most common ones.

Why do we need to change?

"A bad system will beat a good person every time." - W. Edwards Demming

Your organisation is already entering into contracts every day, and good, hard-working people are no doubt doing their best to deliver what is needed. People understandably can be reluctant to consider whether what their team produces might be improved—it can easily be taken as suggesting that they are incompetent.

Although we see a lot of lawyering heroics, the bottom line is that the performance of an organisation's contracting will be a function of its overall contracting system, in the broad sense, including its processes, tools, team behaviour, and leadership.

Moving the conversation from individual performance to system performance has two advantages:

- It will make it easier to discuss results and possible improvements; it's no longer personal.
- If you focus on the performance of the system, you have a fighting chance of making it better.

So the answer to the challenge of "why change", comes down to: how well is the contracting system achieving the overall objectives of the organisation? I don't know how your organisation is doing, but 91% of the executives responding to the WorldCC Benchmark Report 2023 considered improving their organisations commercial and contracting capabilities to be important.

How do we know it will work?

"Continuous improvement is better than delayed perfection" - Mark Twain

After you've made the case for the need for change, the next objection is usually to question whether the new approach will work. I'm arguing in this book that the way we deliver contracting needs to radically change and that the traditional ways of supporting contracting can get in the way. Whether you are making changes to how your internal team works or bringing in an ALSP like Radiant Law, questions will be asked—lawyers are sceptical.

Scepticism can be valuable, but has its limits. We can't debate our way to finding better ways of working, we have to try things out and learn from what happens. As I've noted above, we have had too many opinions in contracting and too little data. I've shared case studies and results, but the truth is that you will only know if the approach in this book is right for your organisation by experimenting.

So the answer to the question of how we know it will work is: let's give it a go and see. This underlines the value of iterative improvements over major transformation projects. You not only get going faster, you also de-risk the impact if what you try doesn't work. Don't hand over all of your contract support to an untested third party, instead run a pilot to see how it goes for some initial contracts. Don't rush to automate everything with a CLM, instead use simple tools that you can change later. Most importantly, don't get stuck, trying to prove in advance, things that can only be tested in practice.

What about my role?

"What's dangerous is not to evolve." - Jeff Bezos

Our experience is that both in-house teams and traditional law firms have over emphasised seniority when handling contracts. It's understandable why: if you don't invest in making tacit knowledge explicit, you are going to have to rely on team members seeing enough examples to build their own mental model from scratch.

Experience can be used as a shield against a deeper concern: if someone with less experience can do this work, what am I going to do? This concern doesn't just materialise in claims that everything is complex; it also appears in the creation of complexity. Turgid templates, byzantine processes, things needing to be bespoke or positions always being case-by-case, are all symptoms of an understandable fear of redundancy.

The answer to this concern is not to dismiss the need for experience, it's to focus on where it adds the most value. Complex, strategic deals will often throw up novel issues and deep experience is invaluable. Making judgement calls on hard issues on the simpler deals is also needed. Building assets and leading change projects that can be used by others is a force multiplier for the broader team. Working closely with the business to deliver strategic goals plays to the strength of embedded in-house lawyers, and it doesn't have to just be deals. This work is not only more likely to be recognised by the business as adding strategic value, but also more interesting. The problem we have in contracting is not enough thinking, not a lack of need for thinking. Those who are willing to let go of the perceived safety of churning deals to tackle the more ambiguous and higher-value strategic work will always be in demand.

Summary

I've explored how to divide up your contracts by complexity and frequency, and the approaches available to supporting each category. Over time the goals should be simplification, empowering the business, and appropriately resourcing the contracts where the business will still need help.

This approach will inevitably lead to questions, and I suggested how I would answer questions such as why the need for change, how will we know it works, and what about my role? The most important point is that simplifying contracting does not mean dumbing it down. We need to be more thoughtful in how we approach contacting and those willing to deploy their expertise to making contracting better, not just more complex, will be rightfully in demand.

Chapter 10 The Future of Contracting

I am wary of futuristic takes on contracting, as the problems we face come from not doing the basics, and many of the solutions we need are available here and now. I've addressed AI, but if I don't at least mention blockchain and smart contracts, then some readers will feel cheated, and how can I resist doing a drive-by on these topics? So here goes.

The blockchain continues to be a solution looking for a problem, and despite all the hype to date, it has failed to demonstrate much value in the world of contracting that cannot be delivered using far simpler solutions. The problems we have are as mundane as not finding contracts, rather than fraud, and there are more straightforward ways of solving a fraud problem without needing blockchain. Therefore, I predict that there will not be far-reaching use of blockchain technology in commercial contracting within the next thirty years (my working horizon). Still, we will continue to be nagged by the sellers of snake oil.

I also predict that smart contracts (that is, contracts running as code on a blockchain as opposed to computable contracts, which I'll discuss below) will fail to get widespread traction for two reasons:

- First, smart contracts will likely turn out to have few practical use cases, given their limited ability to affect the real world. Yes, they can release cryptocurrency funds from escrow, but has anyone checked with a CFO about the desirability of locking up material sums in escrow? If the program can't control the world, then the smart contract's core point is defeated.

- Second, there are fundamental problems with applying computational reasoning to a messy world.[111]

Much of the world will continue to be eaten by software, as noted by Silicon Valley supremo Marc Andreessen. Some actions previously controlled by contracts will instead be controlled by code. Still, I don't expect smart contracts to play a significant role.

Finally, I explained in Chapter 5 why I don't think AI, even GenAI, will be able to fully automate the contracting process. It's use cases are increasing, though, so I encourage you to experiment with where it might help. We will still have to do the basics set out in this book (good luck with getting a computer to interpret a contract you can't find!), and there will be more mileage in writing clear contracts than in waiting for a machine to reliably decipher legalese.

If the blockchain, smart contracts, and AI won't significantly transform contracting, what will be different? If past performance is anything to go by, progress will probably continue to be slow, but there are three themes that I hope to see more of, above and beyond a wider adoption of the RADICAL approach to contracting. Those three themes are the human dimension, abstraction, and computability.

It's all about humans

In all the talk of applying technology to contracting, it's easy to forget that this is about relationships, even if they are commercial relationships, and therefore about humans. Ultimately, relationships are between people, and it is people who will decide whether to invest in one or let it wither. You must get people to agree with you and to value what you offer. It is people who experience the

---

[111] Sean McGrath has written a brilliant seventeen-part series on the computational challenges that come from the inherent ambiguities in law and contracts. All of it is worth reading, although parts 16 and 17 particularly focus on smart contracts. https://seanmcgrath.blogspot.com/2017/03/what-is-law-part-1.html.

contracting process that you create, not machines. The endgame should not be fully automated trading systems but humans building relationships with other humans to add value for humanity[112].

As we enthuse about innovation and increasing automation, let's spare a thought for the user experience. We need to be designing processes that are delightful for all the participants, including the other side, and that embrace the contracting function's role in marketing your company. Remember that humans don't create relationships with technology[113].

Right now, too many parties get to experience "computer says no" through monolithic standard terms, unreasonable contracting policies, and teams who refuse to engage with the other side, all of which boils down to corporate-scale bloody-mindedness.

Abstraction

In computer science, "abstraction" is used to hide the less important details to reduce complexity. Over time, programmers have created "higher level" programming languages and tools that let them focus on business logic, ignoring how the computer works underneath. As abstraction has increased over time, programming has become much faster and programmers more productive[114].

---

[112] I mentioned "relational contracting" earlier—the furthest end of the transactions-relationships spectrum. This approach focuses on building early trust and collaboration through an exploratory model of negotiation that emphasises growing the pie and adapting to changing circumstances. I have included an article in the Reading List at the end of this book, if you are interested in learning more.

[113] With the possible exception of Apple's customers.

[114] It also means that software typically runs slower but increasing computing power has more than made up for this.

We need a similar approach in contracting. We spend too much time in the weeds, forcing business users to engage with impenetrable contracts that obfuscate the essential points. Those of us who are experts in the law have created a dependency that means we have to be involved and consulted to make sense of contracts and implement them safely.

While there will always be a need for specialist advice, I expect to see systems emerge that empower business users to run most, if not all, of the contracting process themselves. These systems will provide guidance and guardrails to allow the users to focus safely on the business issues and not on the contractual language itself. The challenge with these systems is that they typically require both parties to change their behaviours and drop Word and email, so we can safely assume that this won't happen any time soon. I expect the parties will need to move to a neutral third-party platform that allows them to choose between negotiation options to minimise the need for free-form drafting. And if you can do this, then you can move to data-centric contracts.

Data-centric and computable contracts

Contracting is currently overwhelmingly document-centric. Even if it never gets printed out, a typical contract is made up of one or more documents with little, if any, structure to the critical data points. Departments must revisit agreements regularly and spend fortunes reviewing them to deal with the latest regulatory change.

This is hardly practical, and as suggested in Chapter 8, a good start would be to stop throwing data away. But consider this thought experiment: if you were to build a sufficiently complex document automation template that covered the majority of the negotiation points that arise in practice[115] (a large but still finite set of options), then the outcome of any negotiation could be represented mostly, if not totally, as data—in particular, the options selected. If you could store that data as a representation of the contract, then you would just need to interrogate that data to answer questions about what is lurking in your contract portfolio. This is what I mean by data-centric contracting.

A data-centric approach would still require you to read the contract's language to answer questions. Some of these questions (often relating to financial provisions) might best be answered by representing the agreed position not just as data but modelled as actual code. Not all provisions in an agreement lend themselves to being encoded, and with this approach, there would still need to be a human-readable version of the deal. The advantage of code is that the contract (or rather the coded representation) would answer questions about different scenarios, allowing sophisticated modelling across portfolios. We call these contracts computable or Ricardian agreements, not to be confused with the smart contracts loved by blockchain-boosters, where the contract is the code (with all the problems I highlight above).

Computable contracts are an attractive concept for financial institutions, which spend significant resources on modelling derivatives and other financial instruments and have led the way in developing this approach. At least one of the leading insurance and asset management groups have a board-backed initiative to make their core products computable. I expect that this will spread in the future.

---

[115] Oliver Hart and Bengt Holmström won the Nobel Prize for Economics in 2016 for their theory of incomplete contracts. They rightly note that a contract cannot cover all contingencies. That doesn't mean that a system can't handle the most common points that come up in negotiations.

To implement computable contracts, you will need most of this book's steps and you'll have to adopt the abstraction approach[116]. As warned early on in the no-silver-bullets section, completeness will also be a challenge. It won't happen soon, but it will put the power back in the end-user's hands, so I think it's worth pursuing[117].

Summary

Although there is much that lawyers bring to the contracting process, I am a firm believer in the potential of empowering our end-users to do more, with lawyers (leveraging technology) focusing on the more complex transactions and creating the systems that will empower the business. As we do this, it will be a terrible mistake if we focus on the automation and not the relationships we are trying to create. Relationships are ultimately between humans, so our future systems need to create spaces for better, more informed communication, not more opportunities for computers to say no. I'm optimistic, but there is plenty to do first to get the basics in place.

---

[116] Because negotiations will need to be limited to predetermined options as no one is going to want to rewrite code as part of a negotiation.

[117] The observant reader will note that I have raised a couple of serious objections in this book to such a system. It would need to support discussions between humans since relationships are ultimately between humans, and it assumes that for at least some types of deals, the system could be complete enough to be practical. It would also have to be built on commonly accepted terms, which are still the exception although they are starting to emerge. I think it's possible, but difficult.

Conclusion

And that's it! Not everything there is to know about fixing your contracting, of course, but a framework to help you prioritise, focus on what matters, and get going.

Reading about it is the easy part; doing it takes time. As you get started, try to tame your inner perfectionist and use the "good enough for now" test. You're not going to make constant progress and you will be overwhelmed at times with the day-to-day work, but that's OK. Come back to it when you're ready, and know that there is help at hand if you need it. Remember, as you put the pieces in place, the day-to-day work will get easier.

To be successful, you will need to bring your team and then the broader business on the journey to adopt these new ways of working. The whole team doesn't have to change at once. You can start with the early adopters and sweep up the laggards later. For this to work, though, you will need management support for the changes and a more balanced approach between risk and speed. Start in one part of your organisation, show the benefits, and bring the others with you.

One reviewer of this book wondered if most teams will do something and then stall. Perhaps, but it doesn't have to be that way. The three things that have helped us keep going are:

- **Leadership attention**: Ongoing change requires consistent attention from the top that recognises that there will be times when everyone is too busy but keeps applying (reasonable) pressure.

- **Time**: Leaders also need to provide support. Most importantly, continuous improvement is real work and will take time. Give the team that time. Otherwise, change won't happen.

- **Cadence**: Create a rhythm of regular meetings, challenges and reporting back. After a while, the team will just accept change as part of business-as-usual!

Once the team has adopted this approach as a habit, you'll wonder how you ever managed it before. If you would like someone to apply the RADICAL approach to your lower-risk common contracts, we would love to talk.

About Radiant Law

Radiant Law is an award-winning UK law firm with teams in London, Cape Town, Johannesburg, Trinidad, and Malaysia helping some of the world's largest companies with their contracts. We combine fixed pricing (to give our clients price certainty and align interests), legal judgement, design, data analysis, Lean, and technology to help our clients fix their contracting problems and create great relationships. We are also a certified B Corp, a new kind of business that balance purpose with profit to build an inclusive and sustainable economy that works for everyone.

Radiant Law has won the FT Innovative Lawyers' award for Pioneer Law Firm of the Year, Law.com's ALSP of the Year, The Lawyer's Law Company of the Year, and the Managing Partners Forum's Mould-Breaking Firm of the Year. We are acknowledged as one of the global leaders of a new type of law firm, appearing in books such as ***Tomorrowland: Scenarios for Law Firms Beyond the Horizon*** (Bruce McEwan, 2017), ***Tomorrow's Lawyers: An Introduction to Your Future*** (Richard Susskind, 2013), ***The Rise of Legal Outsourcing: Risk and Opportunity*** (Mary Lacity et al., 2014) and ***The Great Legal Reformation: Notes from the Field*** (Mitch Kowalski, 2017).

How we help our clients:

Contracting Managed Legal Services

We provide end-to-end fixed-price managed legal services to support high volumes of day-to-day contracts, from intake and triage to drafting, negotiation, the approvals process, and signature.

Contract Projects

We deliver large-scale contract review and update projects, including support for regulatory changes to fix existing contracts or to transfer them as part of a business sale or outsourcing.

Next steps

There are several resources to help you get going on your contracting improvement journey:

Optimised Contracting Assessment

The Radiant Law Optimised Contracting Assessment helps you measure where you are on the contracting journey and what to prioritise next. The Assessment is a free to use tool, and you will receive a customised report.

Visit: www.radiantlaw.com/scorecard

Contracting Workshops

We hold regular free live workshops explaining RADICAL contracting and the 3Rs improvement approach.

Visit: www.radiantlaw.com/workshop

Contracting Guides

We have published multiple free guides and resources for improving the contracting process.

Visit: www.radiantlaw.com/resources

Get in touch

I wish you the best of luck as you tackle your contracting process. I would love to hear how you do, and if you ever want to ask questions or share experiences, you can find me here:

Email: alex.hamilton@radiantlaw.com

Twitter: @alexhamiltonrad

LinkedIn: linkedin.com/in/alexhamilton/

Web: radiantlaw.com

The Author

Alex Hamilton

Alex trained as a lawyer, working at Norton Rose and Shaw Pittman (now Pillsbury Winthrop Shaw Pittman) before making partner at the global US firm Latham & Watkins, where he specialised in outsourcing and complex technology deals and co-chaired the global Technology Transactions Group. After a Jerry Maguire-like moment where he wrote a mission statement (not a memo) to the executive committee in 2009 calling for more innovation[118], he left to found Radiant Law in 2011.

Alex has worked in London and New York and is qualified to practice English and New York law. He has negotiated some of the largest outsourcing deals worldwide and has led seven projects ranked in the FT Innovative Lawyers awards. He is a fellow of the College of Law Practice Management, a Shingo Alumni, and was a finalist for the FT's Legal Innovator of the Year Award. Alex is a regular public speaker about contracting improvements, legal tech, and the changing legal industry and has been known to share one or two opinions on these topics on Twitter and LinkedIn.

Alex is now the CEO of Radiant Law, which means that he doesn't do many deals any longer but does get to lead a team of lawyers, developers, engineers, data analysts, and designers in reinventing legal services. This has turned out to be even more fun.

---

[118] https://alexhamiltonrad.tumblr.com/post/78751332144/innovation-opportunities

Acknowledgements

First edition

Many people helped make this book possible. For starters, our clients who backed us and the Radiant Law team who figured out how to make contracting fly, one contract at a time. It's been a hell of a journey working with you all over the past ten years. Greg Tufnell and Serena Wallace-Turner, without whom Radiant Law would have been just another also-ran. All the people who so generously reviewed and commented on this book—the wrong-headed opinions and mistakes remain mine, the credit for the smarter points is all theirs: Ken Adams, Paul Boyle, Peter Carayiannis, Martin Clausen, Professor Norman Faull, Ken Grady, Sol Irvine, Professor Richard Moorhead, Denis Potemkin, Ian Teague, and Duc Trang. World Commerce and Contracting, who led the way in applying rigour and empiricism to contracting. Vita Hamilton, Maeve MacGlinchey, Verity Ridgman, and Susan Ryan for their brutally tough editing. Bill Bonney of Last Mile Publishing, Ada Hamilton, Tim Hamilton, Dawn Hapgood, Nicola Lyons, and Mykola Shelepa for their excellent eyes as we agonised over the artwork and layout. It's good to be surrounded by people who care so much about the details. And finally, Nonku Nyathi for her abiding support and patience as I paced up and down, trying to get the ideas straight in my head.

Thank you all.

Second edition

There have been many wonderful conversations since the first edition came out, and many of the people named above have continued to help me think through how we can make contracting better. Others who have helped include Catherine Bamford, Chris

Butterworth, Jeff Carr, Doug Dawson, Casey Flaherty, Jamie Gannaway, Daniel Hoadley, Nicola Jones, Damien Riehl, Ronald Ross, Nicola Shaver, Alex Smith, Elizabeth de Stadler, Andy Unger, and Andy Wishart. As before, the wrong-headed opinions and mistakes remain mine. Another shout-out to WorldCC - Tim Cummins and Sally Guyer are showing the world a better way. The Radiant Law team continue to do the hard yards to delight our clients and make their contracting fly - it is an honour to work with you all. Jess Gowar, Nicola Lyons, Ian Teague, Greg Tufnell, and Serena Wallace-Turner have been critical to Radiant Law's continued success, helping create the context in which Radiant's team-led decision making can work. Michelle Aspeling, Tim Hamilton, and Mykola Shelepa helped make this book fit for publication, and Dad has also been the best cheerleader one could hope for. Above all, we would be nothing without our clients who have continued to back us, shared their needs and feedback (generally positive), taken a punt on a new type of legal provider, and supported our perpetual experiments.

The second edition of this book was written at a time when behaviour in the legal world is under particular scrutiny. There are many who are part of the movement to do the right thing, but I want to acknowledge some friends who are making a difference: Ciaran Fenton, Paul Gilbert, Richard Given, Professor Richard Moorhead, Jennifer Swallow, and Ben White.

Finally, none of this would have been possible without the support of Jenny Hamilton, who I miss deeply.

Thank you all.

Further Reading

Ken Adams. ***A Manual of Style for Contract Drafting***
5th ed, American Bar Association, 2023
The definitive guide to drafting clearer contracts.

Niklas Modig and Pär Åhlström. ***This is Lean***
Rheologica Publishing, 2012
A great introduction to Lean principles, underlining that it is more than a set of tools.

Gerald Langley, Ronald Moen, Kevin Nolan, Thomas Nolan, Clifford Norman, Lloyd Provost. ***The Improvement Guide***
2nd ed, Jossey-Bass, 2009
A comprehensive guide to process improvement, following the Lean approach.

Douglas Hubbard. ***How to Measure Anything***
3rd ed, Wiley, 2014
A practical primer on how to make better decisions and apply statistics to your data.

Douglas Hubbard. ***The Failure of Risk Management***
2nd ed, Wiley, 2020
An introduction to how to do risk management right.

Mike Rother. ***Toyota Kata***
McGraw-Hill, 2009
The introduction to the Toyota Kata, an exercise for building scientific thinking in your team.

Marc Stickdorn, Markus Edgar Hormess, Adam Lawrence, Jakob Schneider.
This is Service Design Thinking
BIS Publishers, 2014

This is Service Design Doing
O'Reilly Media, 2016
Introduced the world to service design thinking (and doing).

Steve Krug.
Don't Make Me Think, Revisited
3rd ed, New Riders, 2014
Rocket Surgery Made Easy
New Riders, 2009
Written originally for website user testing, the principles hold for any form or system you ask end-users to adopt.

Lou Downe. ***Good Services***
BIS Publishers, 2020
A practical guide to the fundamental principles for improving (particularly online) services.

W. Edwards Deming. ***Out of the Crisis***
MIT Press, 1982
A guide to how organisations (and their approach to systems and processes) need to be rethought.

Roger Fisher and William Ury
Getting to Yes
3rd ed, Baker and Taylor, 2011
Getting Past No
Random House, 1992
The original guides to principle-led negotiations.

Atul Gawande. ***The Checklist Manifesto***
Profile, 2011
A terrific introduction to why checklists matter and why professionals are dangerous without them.

Eliyahu Goldratt. ***The Goal***

3rd ed, Routledge, 2004
The introduction to the theory of constraints, which is a core underpinning to improving processes.

David Frydlinger, Oliver Hart and Kate Vitasek
A New Approach to Contracts
Harvard Business Review, September 2019
An introduction to relational contracting.

James Womack and Daniel Jones
Lean Thinking
Simon & Schuster, 2003

Lean Solutions
Simon & Schuster, 2005
Two books focused on Lean, including banishing waste and viewing producers and customers as one system. Lean Solutions is more services focused.

Duc V. Trang. ***Architecture of Deals***
Academy Publishing, 2019
Introduces a framework for applying core economic concepts to transactions, explaining some important mechanisms in deals.

Caroline Jarrett and Gerry Gaffney. ***Forms that Work***
Morgan Kaufmann, 2008
A practical guide to making usable forms that will transform how you think about collecting information.

Art Smalley. ***Four Types of Problems***
Lean Enterprise Institute Inc, 2019
How to apply Lean methodologies to solving different types of problems.

Jeffrey K. Liker and Karyn Ross. ***The Toyota Way to Service***

Excellence: Lean Transformations in Service Organizations
McGraw-Hill Education, 2016
Applying Lean to service organisations.

Dr Morgan L. Jones, Chris Butterworth, Brenton Harder. 4 + 1: ***Embedding a Culture of Continuous Improvement in Financial Services***
Action New Thinking Limited, 2018
Applying the Shingo Model to service organisations.

Index

Illustrations

List of Case Studies

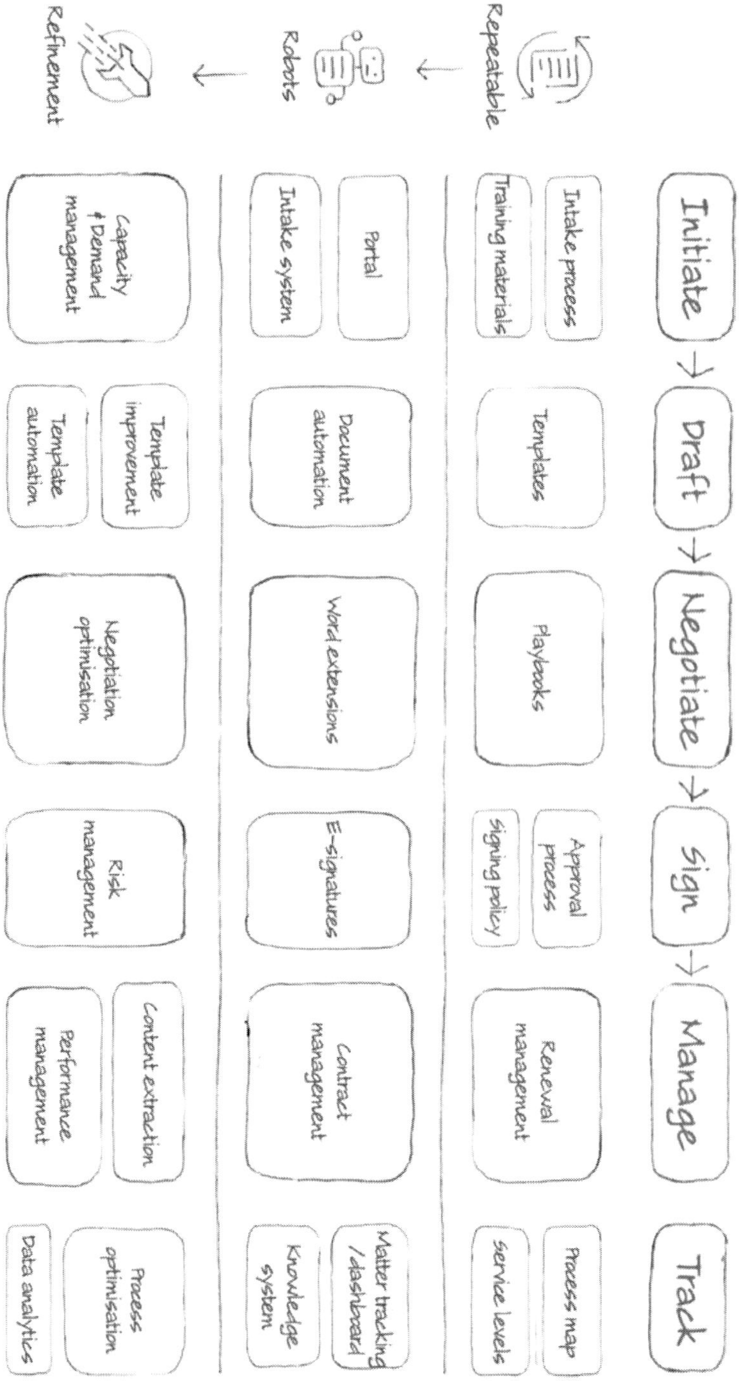

Initiate
Draft
Negotiate
Sign
Manage
Track
Repeatable
Robots
Refinement
Intake process
Training materials
Templates
Playbooks
Approval process
Signing policy
Renewal management
Process map
Service levels
Portal
Intake system
Document automation
Word extensions
E-signatures
Contract management
Matter tracking /dashboard
Knowledge system
Capacity & Demand management
Template improvement
Template automation
Negotiation optimisation
Risk management
Content extraction
Performance management
Process optimisation
Data analytics

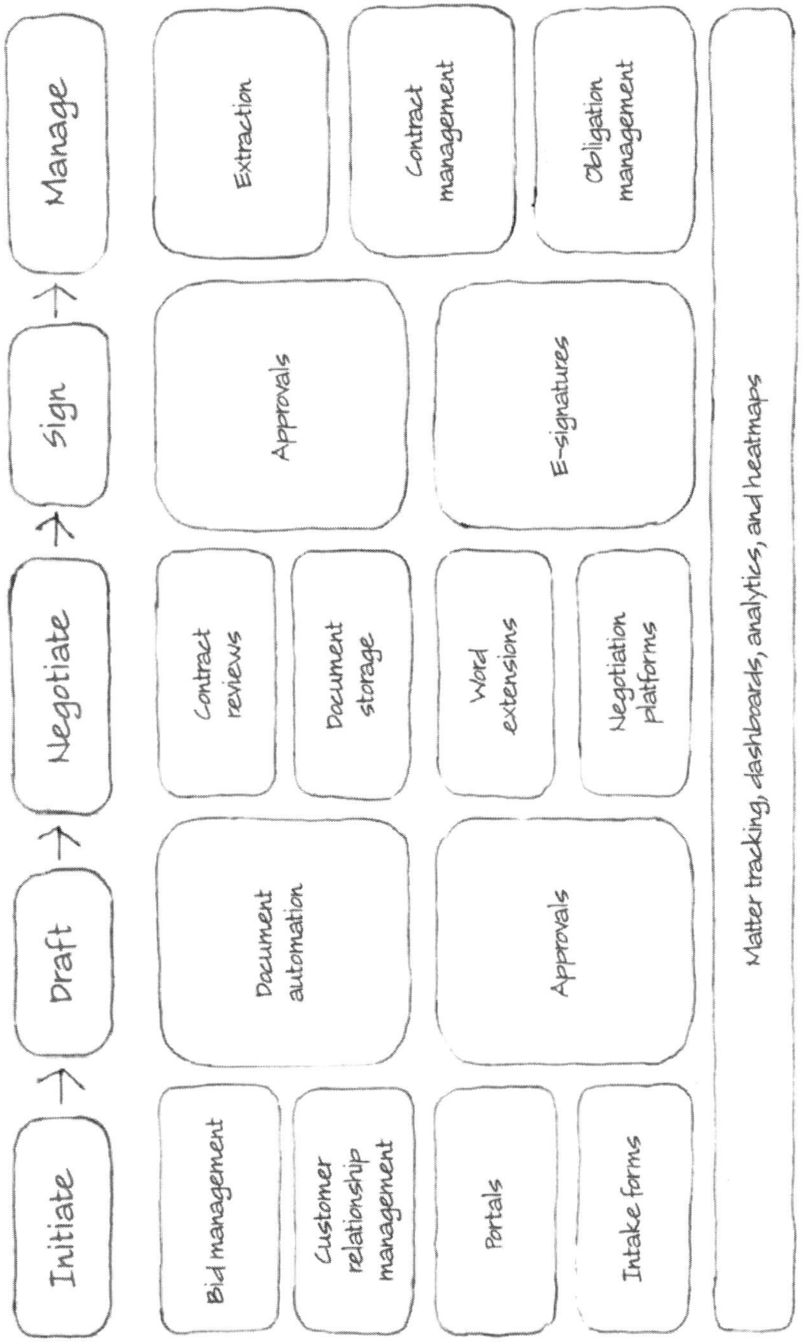
Initiate
Draft
Negotiate
Sign
Manage
Bid management
Customer relationship management
Portals
Intake forms
Document automation
Approvals
Contract reviews
Document storage
Word extensions
Negotiation platforms
Approvals
E-signatures
Extraction
Contract management
Obligation management
Matter tracking, dashboards, analytics, and heatmaps

Printed in Great Britain
by Amazon

48393564R00128